# Regulatory Intelligence 101

By Meredith Brown-Tuttle, RAC

ISBN: 978-0-9673115-0-0

RAPS Global Headquarters
5635 Fishers Lane
Suite 550
Rockville, MD 20852
USA

**RAPS.org**

# Table of Contents

# Table of Contents

## Figures and Graphics

## Tables

# Introduction

At the 2001 RAPS Annual Conference, I attended a session that included a presentation on a regulatory intelligence (RI) database and everything it allowed a regulatory professional to do. My curiosity was sparked, and I went to the vendor hall to learn more about the software. I found not only that software but also several others and decided to investigate what RI was and whether it was something that would interest me. I searched the literature and could find no references on the subject, except the aforementioned presentation. Not letting that stop me, I interviewed people experienced in the profession and found that part of my current job function, the fun part of working as a regulatory associate, was RI, but now it had a name. Thus began my journey and love of RI. RI allowed me to combine my curiosity, research skills and analytical skills with my experience in the pharmaceutical and device industries.

This book is the culmination of my 14-year love affair with RI, a field that has allowed my affinity for regulatory and love of the profession to shine through. It reflects the contributions to the growth and development of RI through the years, and I am proud to have been a part of the process. Initially, this book had 22 authors and

was to have a more international perspective. However, the economic downturn impacted authors' ability to contribute. Because I wanted to make sure this book was available to people who craved more information about RI, I have put together the first edition. I want to extend many thanks to the Drug Information Association's US and EU Regulatory Intelligence Network Group members who contributed to the initial outlines, including, but not limited to (I deeply apologize if I have forgotten anyone):

- Daniel Albahari
- Gesine Bejeuhr
- Kimberly Belsky
- Neal Birkett
- Bertrand Borie
- Linda Bowen
- Brooke Casselberry
- Brad Carte
- Anita Fenty
- Elisabeth Fournier-Qezari
- Helle-Mai Gawrylewski
- Amy Grant
- Kevin Hollister
- Mary Howkins
- Mary Jarosz
- Angelika Joos
- Barbara Kolb
- Christine Mayer-Nicolai

- Brian Mayhew
- Munish Mehra
- Alan Minsk
- Lanchi Nguyen
- Mary Overland
- Tom Perrone
- Cecilia Potez
- Sarah Powell
- Marianne Koehne
- Mike Spitz
- Merete Schmiegelow
- Meeta Vete
- Diane Whitworth
- Xin Min Yue

This book is intended to be a comprehensive tome for those in RI or who want to join the profession. RI is dynamic, and the tools and processes change over time. As such, I cannot claim to be an expert on everything; authors are welcome to contribute to a chapter or add a new one, with an international focus, in the second edition. Please send all contribution requests to: theregulatorium@gmail.com.

## Dedication

Most importantly, I want to thank Linda Bowen, the "regulatory intelligence guru," for her friendship, intelligence, wisdom and words of encouragement in helping develop this book. We have been swapping ideas and slides since we met in 2005, and through our relationship, I have grown as a professional and thank her for that.

CHAPTER 1

# The 5 Ws and H of Regulatory Intelligence

## What This Book Covers

*"An organization's ability to learn, and trans-
late that learning into action rapidly, is the
ultimate competitive advantage."* Jack Welch

Often, the regulatory intelligence (RI) professional feels like a regulatory journalist
for the company he or she works for. If not
writing an article for a newsletter, he or
she might be writing a summary of newly
passed legislation, a guidance document,
a hot topic, putting together a regulatory
strategy or perhaps pulling together the
answer to a research question. All of these
activities involve locating the five Ws and
the H:

- Who?
- What?
- Where?
- Why?
- When?
- How?

Since RI professionals operate by the
above deduction principles, this chapter
covers RI basics, based on answering the
five Ws and the H.

## What?

RI has been done in some way, shape or
form since regulatory was formally recognized as a profession in the US in the late
1970s. At that time, it was considered part
of a regulatory affairs professional's job
and was limited to surveillance of newly
issued regulations and guidance documents. RI presentations started appearing
at formal professional meetings around
2000. Acceptance of RI as a separate function in regulatory has gained momentum
since that time, as the need and benefits
have been realized by drug and device
companies alike.

So what is RI? As is the case with all
great regulatory questions, the answer is,
"It Depends." It depends on the person;
the company; the drug, device or biologic
focus; and the individual's background,
experience, training and familiarity with
the subject matter.

Per the RING (Regulatory Intelligence
Network Group), a Drug Information
Association (DIA) working group in the
Regulatory Affairs Community, RI is
defined as:

> "The act of gathering and analyzing
> publicly available regulatory informa-
> tion. This includes communicating
> the implications of that information,

**Table 1-1. More Definitions**

| Term | Definition |
|---|---|
| Regulatory Information | • can be oral, written, published, unpublished data<br>• basic building blocks of intelligence, the raw information |
| Intelligence | • capacity to acquire knowledge (facts)<br>• experiences (life lessons)<br>• ability to apply life lessons |
| Intelligence vs. Information | • intelligence—active and related to analysis and surveillance<br>• Information—raw data used to create intelligence |
| Strategy | • *Merriam-Webster Medical Dictionary (2002)*—an adaptation or complex of adaptations (as of behavior, metabolism, or structure) that serves or appears to serve an important function in achieving evolutionary success<br>• regulatory strategy—adaptation a company makes to move its product from development to marketing approval<br>• regulatory strategy—incorporates the drug development plan, precedence, an outstanding issue or question, background information, regulations and/or guidance documents, strategic advice, lifecycle management and recommendations on implementation |
| What RI is Not | • competitive intelligence<br>• proprietary information<br>• sales or marketing information<br>• drug pricing or insurance information<br>• reimbursement issues<br>• business intelligence<br>• regulatory information |

and monitoring the current regulatory environment for opportunities to shape future regulations, guidance, policy, and legislation."

The EU RING group (the European Regulatory Intelligence Network Group), has defined RI as:
"Regulatory intelligence is the act of processing targeted publicly available information and data from multiple sources, analysing the data in its relevant context and generating a meaningful output—e.g., outlining risks and opportunities—to the regulatory strategy."

RI is the fun part of regulatory. This is where the professional interprets and analyzes data.

To get a clear picture of RI, it is necessary to know what RI is not, specifically the difference between information and intelligence.

### Other Names for RI

RI has been called by other names, such as:
- regulatory policy
- regulatory strategy
- regulatory affairs
- regulatory relations
- FDA liaison
- regulatory information and intelligence
- regulatory intelligence
- scientific information
- regulatory intelligence and policy
- regulatory strategist
- global regulatory sciences informatics
- scientific and regulatory intelligence
- policy, intelligence and education
- reference librarian

RI is not an oxymoron. But no matter the name, it almost always is the same—analysis of data to create actionable RI.

### What are the differences in RI for drug, device and biologic companies?

- sources of information differ
- surveillance resources differ
- consultants used differ

However, the analysis of information is similar and the goal is the same—approval of marketing applications.

### What does RI provide for regulatory and its customers?

- information for product teams (research and development issues)
- development of executive strategy
- commenting and shaping policy and influencing legislation
- tracking legislation
- tracking approvals, nonapprovals and withdrawals
- compliance
- knowledge management
- training
- creation of corporate policy

RI also allows a company to:
- develop a strategy for a product
- create a development plan for a product
- predict review times for product approvals
- research past precedents and adjust for current regulatory climate
- advise personnel
- write or construct a marketing application incorporating all agency requirements
- adjust a marketing application to ex-US needs
- anticipate questions from the agency based on previous interactions and Advisory Committee Meeting outcomes

RI is different because traditional regulatory focus has been more on product submissions and approvals and less on influencing policy, participating in trade associations, monitoring the landscape or anticipating regulatory changes.

### What typical topics are covered by the RI group?

- country-specific guidance documents, regulations and directives (current, draft or revoked)
- product classification
- marketing applications and the approval process
- Good Clinical Practice (GCP)
- investigator inspections, disqualifications and debarments
- Good Manufacturing Practices (GMPs)
- Quality System Regulations (QSRs)
- computer systems validation, electronic records and signatures
- packaging and labeling
- reporting and recordkeeping
- export/import legislation
- promotion and advertising
- pricing
- pharmacovigilance
- complaint handling, management and reporting
- inspections, inspection outcomes (483s) and outcomes management
- traceability requirements
- Warning Letters
- Establishment Inspection Reports (EIRs)
- product recalls
- product withdrawals
- Refuse to File Letters (or press releases)

### What are the benefits of RI?

- increased compliance
- increased likelihood of marketing application approval
- shortened time from filing to approval
- increased efficiency
- optimized study design to meet regulatory endpoints
- optimized messaging about product benefit
- maximized target market potential (broader indications)

## Why?

RI is the evolution of the regulatory profession, from producing submissions to supporting a product through the complete product development process. The RI function empowers a company with knowledge about the ever-changing regulatory landscape and gives it a competitive edge over those that do not employ RI.

### Why is RI important?

RI also allows a company to:
- increase the likelihood of marketing application approval, by understanding the health agency requirements and reviewing past precedent
- increase the efficiency of planning, creating and updating a product strategy for executing a drug development plan
- provide the regulatory professional with information to:
  o identify opportunities
    - broader indications, precise preclinical, clinical lifecycle management development programs
    - possibly expand drug exclusivity timeframes
    - expedite development and increase efficiency
    - identify possible pitfalls
    - compliance issues, change in requirements for specific indication
  o predict review times for product and/or changes to product
  o answer specific development questions posed by the team

## Where?

*"If only HP knew what HP knows, we would be three times as profitable."* Lew Platt, former HP CEO

The key to a successful RI career is having a complete toolbox, and knowing where to find the information is half the battle.

The tools the RI professional uses can be free or for-fee, but for-fee tools also will help reach the goal more quickly. Later chapters will explore both the tools and methods to transform the information into intelligence.

RI is not just about information external to the company; it also is about information internal to the company (lessons learned, submissions, labeling and marketing information) and making people aware of that information. What kind of information should be mined? Typically, the RI professional wants to be able to find:
- questions to and responses from health authorities (formal and informal meetings)
- applications submitted—when and to whom (which countries)
- compounds in development
- approved product labeling and advertising

## When?

When should a company implement an RI function? How does the company know the time is right to commit resources that will add value to the company? This depends on how large the company is and whether it values a strategic and competitive edge. If a company wants to be successful in the drug development process, it should employ the RI function at all times to maintain its advantage.

## How?

How is regulatory able to help its team members effectively? The first answer is experience, the second is to know where and how to look for the information and the third is to apply the art of transforming information into actionable regulatory intelligence.

How is actionable RI created? Once the RI professional has the information, it needs to be transformed into something that can be utilized by other team members. RI would include:
- researching the question

**Table 1-2. Typical RI Output**

| Output | What it Could Contain |
|---|---|
| Newsletter or Bulletin | Can be weekly, monthly or quarterly and distributed via email or posted on an intranet site. Provide any and all hyperlinks to original document when available.<br><br>A summary of the following (only about a paragraph in length):<br>• subject matter—CMC, clinical, safety, nonclinical, etc.<br> o proposed or recently codified regulation, directive, guidance document<br> o explanation of how recent information will affect current practice, and proposed changes (if any) to current practices to comply or be in-line with new information<br>• hot topics—give an overview of upcoming or changing legislation (such as biosimilars or the transparency initiatives)<br>• impact of recently attended seminars or meetings |
| Strategy | Overarching development plans, taking into consideration all aspects of product development for a specific indication. To build a product strategy would include reviewing past precedent or predicates, competitor products, press releases, pipeline development by phase and approved product labeling.<br><br>Strategies are a snapshot of the current regulatory, scientific and legislative environment. |
| Recent Drug or Device Approvals | Review of a recent approval package, including: pertinent regulatory history, safety database, nonclinical studies and clinical studies conducted and reviewers' questions and concerns. |
| Research or Answers to Specific Questions | Regulatory research and analysis; providing answers to directed questions. |
| Surveillance | Survey or monitor the global regulatory landscape, looking for changes or proposed changes to official regulatory documents. Output could be in a newsletter, "Hot Topic Bulletin" or special bulletin outlining impact to the company and its products. |
| Profiles | Profiles of the names, publications, education and stance taken by reviewers and Advisory Committee members. |
| Commenting | Company comments or comments provided to a trade association on draft guidance documents. This can be regional or global in nature. |
| FOI Requests | Requested directly from FDA or via a vendor for information available through the *Freedom of Information Act (FOI)*. |
| Advisory Committee Notes | Summary of what took place at a recent Advisory Committee meeting and impact on product development. Also may include information on Advisory Committee members, such as biographies and voting history. |
| Guidance Document Review | In-depth analysis of a new guidance document and its impact on the current development program. |
| Division Review | Review of recent division approvals, looking for emerging trends. |
| REMS Review | Review of all drugs with required REMS, looking for trends and any impact on the development program. |
| Registration Procedures | Outline of how to start a clinical trial or file a marketing application in a specific country or region. |
| Training | Training or "brown bag" lunches on hot topics, how to use the RI department or any other topics of interest. |

- conducting surveillance
- summarizing product approvals
- transforming information into intelligence by analyzing all available information and synthesizing it into a response, strategy or position
- presenting the information to team members in a format usable to them

**Figure 1-1. Regulatory Intelligence Process**

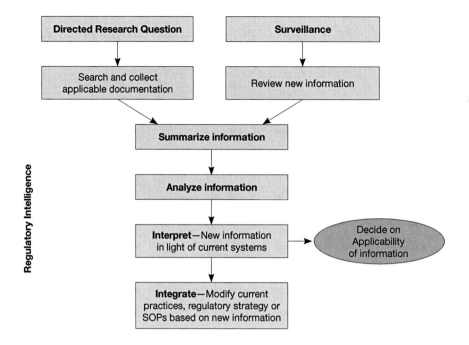

• storing and managing data for future reference

Please see **Figure 1-1** for an overview of the RI process.

## Who?

Who conducts RI is a question each regulatory department needs to answer individually. RI can be done internally by the regulatory department or on an as-needed basis, by a dedicated person or department; or farmed out to a consultant or consulting firm.

What attributes make a good RI analyst? Characteristics of an RI analyst include:

### Regulatory Experience

• long and broad experience
• relationships with other regulatory personnel (network)
• relationships with regulators
• attention to detail

• a complete toolbox to help monitor the landscape and address development issues

### Insight

• sees beyond the apparent
• able to make connections between data that are not always obvious

### Problem Solver

• fits the information pieces together in a meaningful way
• good analytical skills
• curious
• articulate
• clear and unambiguous communications (to the extent possible), including verbal, written and presentation
• able to tailor message to audience
• able to work with other functions outside regulatory
• able to find the information needed

## What department divisions exist within RI?

The typical division of RI activities includes the following:

### *Operations*

- regulatory research
- monitoring and surveillance of the regulatory landscape, including specific therapeutic areas
- drug approvals
- freedom of information (FOI) requests
- newsletters
- hot topics (analysis of regulatory trends)
- training
- Advisory Committee member or reviewer profiles
- knowledge management

### *Strategy*

- regulatory strategy, development plan or therapeutic area analysis for a product
- guidance interpretation and application
- due diligence
- Citizen's Petitions
- participation or observation of Advisory Committee or other public meetings
- identifying regulatory trends and anticipating effect on company and products

- monitoring health authority organizational changes
- white papers or position statements

### *Policy*

- commenting
- government affairs
- trade group participation
- professional associations

Please note there is a strategic component in research, so there is some overlap in the functions, and they are not necessarily as distinct as presented above. The topics above will be explored in individual chapters in more detail.

## Conclusion

RI is an art form and a skill that can be molded when a regulatory professional has a depth and breadth of knowledge and a curious mind. The value RI can bring to a company, as a separate department, is still burgeoning but increasingly becoming more mainstream as companies recognize the value of transforming the multitude of publically available information into actionable and meaningful intelligence and its effect on reducing timelines and budgets.

CHAPTER 2

# The Basic Regulatory Intelligence Toolbox

As when preparing to assemble a new piece of furniture, the RI professional needs to determine which tools will be needed to complete the project—conducting regulatory intelligence requires knowledge about what tools are available, so when the professional is presented with a question, strategy, research or due diligence request, he or she will be aware of potential tools to help answer the questions.

The tools an RI professional will have in his or her toolbox will depend on the company type and whether company leadership recognizes the value and competitive edge RI provides. This chapter includes mirror images of free and for-fee tools, as this typically is the dividing line between small and large company resources. A large company can employ an army of intelligence tools, while the small company scrambles with a volunteer militia. However, the RI process and goal are the same: to be able to track and analyze the regulatory environment and prepare for future obstacles as the company progresses through drug development, aiming for a speedy approval.

In the author's case, no matter where she goes, she tries to have at least the free tools in her RI toolbox because she can get a lot done with very little; however,

having the proper tools to do the jobs saves a lot of time, i.e., the for-fee tools.

## Sources of Regulatory Information

There are numerous sources of regulatory information, but there is no single place to find it all. In addition, to answer a question or develop a strategy, multiple sources might be required to support the position. Sometimes the answers are simple and do not take much research; other times it takes hours of mining through the information for the answer. A good place to start includes these RI common sources:

- regulations, laws and directives
- guidance documents (preamble and comments)
- panel meetings
- previous approvals (past precedence)
- regulatory/health authority websites
- commercially available databases
- health agency publications

However, regulations and guidance documents tell half the story. The above sources provide the black and white facts, while most of the regulatory information and the answers or support being sought are gray. Some examples of gray areas would be if the guidance for a company's product is waived, if there is no guidance at all or if the company's interpretation of guidance is different than the RI professional's previous experience, because interpretation varies by company and experience. Less common regulatory information locations that might provide clues include:

- business intelligence websites and databases
- press releases
- specialized regulatory intelligence software
- compliance guides
- professional and scientific articles
- health authority presentations
- email alerts and newsletters
- competitor information
- regulatory reference and information sites
- educational conferences
- Warning Letters and Untitled Letters
- books and newspapers
- FDA Advisory Committee meeting minutes
- Freedom of Information (FOI) requests
- local chapter meetings of various organizations
- consultants
- interactions with other regulatory professionals or colleague(s)
- interactions with heath authority reviewers

## Undiscovered and Underutilized RI Sources

One of the most important RI skills the RI professional can develop is networking: with sources within his or her department, company and working groups, with a good reference librarian and at trade, industry and professional association meetings. RI professionals should join LinkedIn and get actively involved in discussion groups. After about 20 years in regulatory, there never seem to be any truly new questions (albeit with

nanotechnology, stem cells and gene therapy, this perspective does not apply), just a novel perspective on an old question. If the RI professional does not know the answer or a place to start, the chances are that someone within his or her network will have the answer or provide some guidance on a good place to start.

Those who do not have a network developed yet or need a starting point should see "Regulatory Intelligence Tools: 2012" by Bowen and Brown-Tuttle, *Regulatory Focus*, April 2012, for a comprehensive list of global regulatory information websites that is published on an biennial basis; or see Regulatorium.com for an electronic version of the article.

## Free and For-Fee Tools Comparison

### Top 5 Free Tools

#### Annual RI Tools Article
The author updates this article every other year for *Regulatory Focus*. This article has global links for regulatory agencies, worldwide labels and review links and, most importantly, regulatory information and intelligence providers. When asked a question, the first place the author goes is to the tools article to find the information needed.

#### Clinical Trial Registries
When planning strategy and seeking clinical trial endpoints and patient safety database numbers (especially for orphan products), the author starts her search at Clinicaltrials.gov and further refines her research with Medline/literature reviews and approved drug reviews at Drugs@FDA or European Public Assessment Reports. Examples of clinical trial registries include:
- NIH Clinicaltrials.gov
- EudraCT
- WHO (International Clinical Trials Registry Portal)
- Current Controlled Trials
- IFPMA Clinical Trial Portal
- JAPIC Clinical Trials Information

## FDA.gov or any Other Health Authority Website

When information is needed on regulations, directives, guidance documents, etc., why go anywhere but to the source? Some agency websites are easy to navigate, while others are almost impossible (the format keeps changing, the site is constantly re-launched or the site name is updated, making the previous links invalid). But, health authorities are the publishing source, and their sites have the original documentation that guides drug development. To make it easier to track these websites, most health authorities offer RSS feeds or email alerts to keep RI professionals abreast of the latest changes in the regulatory environment.

## NDA Pipeline Information

Drugs.com is valuable because it consolidates press releases about drugs and FDA activity in one place. It also can provide the international non-proprietary name (INN) and trade name of a drug in international markets.

### FDLI SmartBrief

*FDLI SmartBrief* is a free daily newsletter sponsored by the Food and Drug Law Institute and can be relied on for daily happenings in the world of devices, drugs and biologics (www2.smartbrief.com/news/fdli/index.jsp?brief=FDLI).

## Google

Amazing items can be found via a Google search: a competitor's press release, protocols, an Investigator's Brochure or drugs currently under development. RI professionals should not be afraid to spend the time and drill down to find the information. Sometimes it requires scanning 20 pages, and other times what is needed is on page 2. No other search engine provides the data as quickly as Google. If an RI professional needs a quick informational translation, Google Translate is a great start. However, this website should not be used as a certified translation service for submission purposes.

## Tools, by Subscription Only

### Regulatory Information Databases

The author's database of choice is Tarius (but other providers are available). When asked a question, the author goes to one of the 75+ countries and look for explanatory documents on how to start or maintain a trial, the pertinent guidance documents and associated forms. What really makes life easier is the new Cross Country Table feature that compares and contrasts requirements for clinical trials and marketing authorization (and many more topics) across countries, so clinical trial document requirements can be planned in a matter of minutes, as opposed to days to weeks to read and synthesize all the requirements on a country-by-country basis (not to mention the translation issues). Other RI databases include:

- Thomson Reuters IDRAC Cortellis
- Compliance Control
- Wolters Kluwer Mediregs

Please see Chapter 3 for additional information about Regulatory Intelligence databases.

### Citeline's Trialtrove

It is possible to spend hours looking through listings of clinical trials, mapping out their endpoints and stage of approval. This database covers clinical trial information from global, publically available information and details, in a comparison format, the patient population, stage of development, available products and endpoints. What can take hours with a clinical trial registry is available in minutes with Trialtrove. After using this tool, it is hard to go back to mining information from clinical trial registries.

### PharmaPendium

PharmaPendium has worked with FDA and the EMA to convert every publically available Summary Basis of Approval or European Public Assessment Report (SBA or EPAR, also known as the approval package) to optical character recognition

(OCR) format and made them available in their database. If working on a drug from the 1930s, 1980s or 1990s (before the reviews were posted on the FDA website), it is possible to go to PharmaPendium and retrieve precedent information to support a 505(b)(2) application. Also, when working on a strategy for a new drug and looking to see what drugs have been approved, merely typing in "diabetes" will pull a list of all the reviews that contain the word "diabetes." Using various available filters, all the drugs approved for any type of diabetes can be reviewed in minutes, versus looking through the *Physician's Desk Reference* or trolling the web for the information (and it better prepares the RI professional to work with a physician because he or she is armed with knowledge of treatment modalities in the indication). PharmaPendium also provides information on FDA Advisory Committee documents, Meyler's Side Effects of Drugs and Mosby's Drug Consults.

### NDA Pipeline information Databases

These types of databases show which drugs are in various stages of development and are a compendium of pharmaceutical industry research, development and approval activity. It is possible to search by drug name, therapeutic category, company name and drug approval status from preclinical research to FDA approval (i.e., Phase I, Phase II, etc.) and some even summarize the clinical trial results and when marketing applications were applied for and granted/denied. Some are global, and others discuss market potential, so the company's marketing department may have a subscription already. For an RI professional trying to plan a regulatory strategy, these databases will reveal who is developing a drug, the type of drug and its phase of development. This information also can be found with Google searches and press releases, but these databases quickly provide the information needed to help put together a landscape of drug development for a particular indication; otherwise, it is hit or miss with Google, and some of

the players might be missed. The data are taken from publically available information. Some of the databases are:

- Inteleos
- Thomson Reuters Partnering (formerly IDdb3)
- Citeline Pharmaprojects
- Sagient Research BioMed Tracker
- Springer HealthCare Adis Insight

### DIA or RAPS Subscription

DIA and RAPS provide daily or weekly updates of current global regulatory and development happenings. Typically these are more comprehensive than the free newsfeeds.

## To Spend Money on Tools or Not

Ultimately, the output of RI is the same regardless of the use of free or fee-based tools; the amount of time spent is the real difference. Subscription tools offer a way to do the job much more quickly, compared to the time spent by the RI professional to find, review, analyze and synthesize the information on his or her own, so the investment in the tools ultimately allows the professional to do more in less time. With the subscription services, the needed information can be synthesized and strategies produced within a few days or a week, not weeks.

Without an operating budget of $50K to $500K a year for tools, the RI professional will probably spend that much money in time reviewing documents or hiring, unexpectedly or unbudgeted, a consultant (on an ad hoc basis) or other employees to do the same work, sometimes at a higher overall cost than the initial outlay for the tools. In the race to bring products to market, the subscription fees are worth the cost and the time saved. If a company is serious about being competitive in the global regulated market, it needs to make the investment in regulatory information tools and the people to put together the intelligence. If not, it will trail behind the company that recognizes the value of RI and the competitive advantage it provides.

**References**

Bowen L. and Brown-Tuttle M. "Regulatory
Intelligence Tools Update 2012: Drugs and
Biologics." *Regulatory Focus*, April 2012.

CHAPTER 3

# RI Databases

## What is an RI database?

An RI database is a commercial program that provides its user with seamless and instant access to global regulatory information, such as regulations, guidance documents, directives, etc., without the user having to visit multiple health authority websites for this collective information, and on a platform that allows the user to search a topic across multiple countries quickly (cannot be done with Google). Additional features provide document analyses, such as expert summaries and explanatory documents (that summarize individual country requirements for clinical trials, marketing applications, orphan drug applications, etc.), cross-country tables, summaries of recent drug approvals and Advisory Committee Meetings, which all contribute to an RI analyst's productivity.

## Why is an RI database needed?

A regulatory professional has limited time to read, summarize and amalgamate new information into the company's regulatory paradigm, much less stay current on all the daily changes, produce a newsletter, research a question, make FOI requests, put together a strategy, etc.; however,

utilizing a database can increase job productivity. The databases all have similar benefits (some more than others) to help the RI professional increase his or her productivity (see **Table 3-1** for a comparison between agency website searches and RI databases), including the following:

- regulatory information is available instantly and in one place (not multiple health agency websites); this includes not only regulations, but also laws, guidance documents, *Federal Register* notices, compliance information, manuals of policies and procedures, FDA manuals, summary basis of approvals, product approvals, Warning Letters, establishment inspection reports, inspection observations, etc.
- explanatory documents guide users through an individual country's drug or device registration process
- access to current, revoked and draft documentation and information
- country-specific downloadable forms

**Table 3-1. Time Savings Using an RI Database versus Agency Website**

| Search Criteria | Agency Website | RI Database | Results— Agency Website | Results— RI Database | Time Savings |
|---|---|---|---|---|---|
| Input "transdermal patch validation batch" | • 11 returns, including an SBA, guidance documents and Q&A<br>• For each document, performed screen searches for key word "transdermal" to find relevant information and then "patch" when realized it was abbreviated to "tdp" | • Key documents returned had key terms highlighted in references<br>• Quickly scanned documents and found answer in 10 minutes | Two hours of searching did not produce needed document on agency Website | Found document after three minutes on RI database; answer in another three minutes of searching | At least two hours |
| Clinical Trial regulations, procedures and documents required in 30 countries | • Needed to find the different health agency websites and then use Google translate to find the pertinent clinical trial regulations (not always readily available); assuming the health authority websites existed | Used explanatory documents to compile a table of requirements for clinical trials in 30 different countries | Two weeks (70-80 hours) at least, and this did not include culture-specific information not included in the guidance documents | Eight hours to review and compile the requirements from the explanatory documents and to fill in needed information from regulations that were not in explanatory documents but included in the references | At least 70 hours of time saved, if the cross-country tables had been available at the time, the information would have been instantaneous, saving almost 80 hours of work |

• daily, weekly or monthly email updates of regulatory agency activities

Some RI databases focus only on drugs, while others focus only on devices, and some do a little of both or a comprehensive job of covering both drugs and devices (please see **Tables 3-2–3-5** for a listing of regulatory information and intelligence database providers by product areas).

## What to Look for in an RI Database

What should an RI professional look for in an RI database? Some databases capture the guidance documents, regulations and

directives for one or two countries electronically but do not provide enhanced search capabilities, surveillance or summarization; instead, they are just online versions of the regulations, which provides little or no benefit to the professional who needs to search across all regions and be able to compare requirements quickly via a key word search.

A true RI database is a product that can facilitate finding regulatory information and assist in transforming the information into intelligence, including:

• contains regulations and guidance documents on a global scale (meaning 75+ countries, across drugs and devices) to allow for search and cross-comparison of these requirements

- provides analysis and summary of data to facilitate rapid translation into intelligence (such as cross-country tables, explanatory documents covering the "how to" per the local country requirements, reviewer profiles, Advisory Committee member profiles, guidance document summaries and "hot topic" summaries)

What really distinguishes the intelligence databases from the information providers? Databases that can help with research, surveillance, summarizing, analyzing or integrating regulatory intelligence are integral to an RI analyst's productivity and provide the most benefit. There is some overlap between surveillance, summarizing, analyzing or integrating, and this is described below.

There is a regulatory intelligence database to fit every company size and budget. Most databases are intuitive to use and, therefore, require minimal training.

## Key RI Database Features

Below is an overview of key desirable RI database features and an explanation of them and their value. Benefits of databases include:

- provide the ability to conduct focused research and surveillance, information summaries and integrate specific topics
- provide limited or in-depth analysis of some documents and subjects
- provide worldwide regulatory information (75+ countries)
- provide daily or weekly updates
- central repository to compile, manage and archive information
- regulatory information available instantly to multiple users simultaneously, all on one site (no need to search multiple websites)
- key word or full text searches by country of choice—ability to tag

or bookmark frequent searches and documents
- information structured logically by subject matter
- provide a newsletter on daily, weekly or monthly basis
- access to current, revoked and draft documentation and information
- country-specific downloadable forms

### Research

This is the biggest part of the RI analyst's job, and the database that provides amalgamated information instantly makes the job easier. Examples of how databases can be used for research include the ability to pull up explanatory documents or expert summaries from different countries to understand how to ask for scientific advice in a specific country or to coordinate the same information request across 12 EU countries or to determine how to apply for a marketing authorization in 75+ countries using the cross-country tables. Another part of the research function is the creation of a "Hot Topic" analysis that provides a summary of pending or recently passed legislation or amalgamated information such as "An Overview of Orphan Drug Regulations and Submissions Requirements" across all countries with orphan drug designation programs.

### Surveillance

The ability to conduct surveillance has its own chapter (Chapter 5). Any database that allows the RI professional to tag, bookmark or pre-program key search terms or delivers a daily, weekly or monthly newsletter is important in staying abreast of changes without having to visit health authority websites on a regular basis.

### Summaries

This is a database that offers a summary of documents or new information, such as new guidance documents or regulations, drug approvals, country-specific

**Table 3-2. Overview of RI and Information Database Providers—Drugs and Devices**

| Provider | Contact Information | Product Benefits |
|---|---|---|
| **Thomson Reuters Cortellis™ Regulatory Intelligence, powered by IDRAC®** | www.idrac.com | Cortellis (IDRAC) provides research, surveillance, summarization and analysis, including:<br>• explanatory documents for 70+ countries, including some device summaries<br>• cross-country tables<br>• AdComm Bulletin summarizing Advisory Committee Meetings, background voting, histories and member profiles<br>• Guidance Bulletin summarizing new guidance documents, providing a document summary at your fingertips<br>• Compliance information and inspector profiles<br>• IDRAC is now part of Thomson Scientific, so the database can interface and be integrated with other Thomson products. |
| **MediRegs** | www.mediregs.com | Provides research and surveillance, including:<br>• software available to allow users to link regulatory and standards references in a manufacturer's internal document with the relevant database document<br>• stores searches and alerts users to any new documents that include the search term(s) |
| **Tarius** | www.tarius.com | Provides research, surveillance, summarization, some analysis and integration, including:<br>• explanatory documents, cross-country tables and regulations for 75+ countries<br>• drug and device approvals, Pediatric Investigation Plans, Safety Alerts, Warning Letters, Recalls, Noncompliance Reports<br>• Advisory Committee Meetings, analyzing background materials, summarizing briefing documents and meeting results; member profiles and voting history<br>• breaks down information into logical subject matters<br>• able to organize favorite documents by personal tags<br>• personalized newsletters and alerts on surveillance terms<br>• provides in-line track changes between versions of EU and US guidance documents<br>• links from company's internal documents to regulations are active for all staff members<br><br>Only service that offers comprehensive coverage of both drug/biologic and device/IVD regulations, explanatory documents and cross country tables. |

requirements, Advisory Committee Meetings and reviewer and inspector profiles. Cross-country tables and explanatory documents or expert summaries also fall into this category. Documents that are pre-summarized cut down on research, analysis and summarization time (another example of this is the orphan drug or "hot topic" summary).

These documents should be summaries of information and be free from bias, as bias can affect how this information is interpreted and applied to the question or strategy.

### Impact Analysis

These types of analytical summaries review the impact of new guidance documents or proposed regulations; Advisory Committee Meeting outcomes; typical questions from reviewers, inspectors and Advisory Committee members; inspection outcomes across a discipline (Good Manufacturing Practice (GMP), Good Laboratory Practice (GLP) and Good Clinical Practice (GCP)); approval of a new drug, etc.

**Table 3-3. Overview of RI and Information Database Providers—Drugs**

| Provider | Contact Information | Product Benefits |
|---|---|---|
| Compliance Control | www.compliance-control.com | • breaks down regulations into 30 categories (advertising, training, compliance, etc.), so users can immediately go to the search topic (available in other programs as well)<br>• provides a glossary and definition of terms<br>• can extract regulations in a table format, so they are ready for regulatory assessments<br>• no explanatory documents yet<br>• in its infancy, but geared toward the smaller company, not as many services as other programs, but continually adding new features |

### What's New/Newsletter

Does the database offer a daily email, weekly or monthly newsletters or alerts, or a section within the database labeled "What's New" that contains recent updates to a new regulation, guidance document, etc.? Do these services provide a distinguishing mark on all documents, indicating whether the documents are current, draft or revoked? This can prove invaluable when conducting research, as it sometimes is necessary to go back to the revoked or outdated document for definitions of terms not in current legislation.

### Defined Searches

Most searches on a regulatory agency website return numerous hits, but not all of them are necessarily relevant; this generally is not the case with RI databases. Most RI databases have the ability to do refined searches by key word, subject matter, country or organization and document number (from documents seen on previous searches). Most of the databases have a synonym dictionary for variations in the spelling of words across different countries, to maximize search results. Items returned from a search are categorized as regulations, directives, guidance documents, standards, etc. When a retrieved document is opened, in any category, the search term(s) is highlighted throughout the text. It also is possible to conduct a key word search in any open document. This combination of features alone can shave 30 minutes or more off typical search time.

### Explanatory Documents or Expert Summaries

Explanatory documents or expert summaries guide an RI professional through a country's drug or device registration process, in English, written by in-country experts. They amalgamate the laws, regulations and guidance documents into a succinct summary that can be applied readily in the professional's daily job, to research or a strategy question. Typical summaries include:

- how to start a clinical trial
- how to maintain a clinical trial
- Adverse Event Reporting (pre- and postapproval)
- clinical and marketed product labeling requirements
- Scientific Advice requests
- orphan drug applications
- Accelerated Approval
- Priority Review
- Special Protocol Assessments
- how to construct a marketing application
- how to deal with variations or changes to marketed products
- GMP regulations and stability requirements
- pre- and postapproval fees
- import/export requirements

Included in the summaries are links to the underlying regulations that form the basis of the synopsis. Country-specific explanatory documents can serve as the basis for developing a regulatory filing strategy for that country. These documents

**Table 3-4. Overview of RI and Information Database Providers—Devices**

| Provider | Contact Information | Product Benefits |
|---|---|---|
| **Clinivation Regulatory Intelligence Reports** | www.clinivation.com/worldview/worldview.php | • provides explanatory document for devices only in 65+ countries<br>• consultants are available, for a fee, to answer additional questions not in explanatory documents, if needed<br>• company offers free "webinars" about global regulatory tools and tips |
| **SOFIE Regulatory Intelligence System** | www.graematter.com/?q=products | • connects information from multiple sources to provide a system for monitoring the regulatory environment, including inspections, Warning Letters, debarments, disqualifications, sanctions, recalls, review times, guidance, adverse events and more<br>• device- and US-specific at this time |
| **Emergo Resource Library** | http://www.emergogroup.com/resources | Strictly speaking, this is not a database but a collection of free explanatory documents on a wide variety of topics about global device regulations, including:<br>• free medical device regulatory process charts and approval timelines<br>• medical device market information<br>• Emergo Group videos and pre-recorded webinars<br>• ministry of health websites worldwide<br>• associations and organizations |

are invaluable, providing, at the click of a button, regulatory research that otherwise would have been outsourced to a seasoned consultant or required weeks of trudging through the regulations of each country and allow the RI professional to make a judgment call or decision about a particular country's needs immediately.

The downside to the underlying source documentation referenced in the explanatory documents is when the RI professional speaks only English, and the source document is not published in English by the native country; however, all service providers will translate the document into English for a fee.

## Cross-Country Tables

As product marketing became more global, the need for a high-level summary of the explanatory documents, across countries arose and was addressed by RI database providers. These tables are invaluable tools that can be used to compare and contrast country requirements for almost all of the topics covered in the explanatory documents. If an RI professional needs to know the laws, timelines and document requirements for starting clinical trials in two, 15 or 75 countries, the cross-country table on clinical trials will provide that information instantly.

Why are these tables needed if the explanatory documents are available? It will take the RI professional more time than it is worth to put the information into tables; it is cheaper to purchase the tables and have the provider update them than to update them him- or herself.

### Guidance Bulletin or Summary

This summary provides an overview of FDA and EMA guidance documents, including the history of their development, guidance document contents, links to public comments and a line-by-line comparison to previously released versions of the guidance.

### Advisory Committee Meeting Summary, Tools and Profiles

Some providers offer the following services for FDA's Advisory Committee Meetings:
- Advisory Committee members' profile overviews
- online repository of all FDA meeting documents
- background analyses of meetings
- briefing summaries
- meeting summaries and results

Why is this valuable? Advisory Committee meeting packages and background information can be 300 to well over 1,000 pages in length; the summary condenses it into pertinent facts and provides potential impact on guidance documents, approvals, etc. It also includes information on the drug development history or approval and valuable competitive intelligence. When looking at the impact of an Advisory Committee Meeting on the company's current program and planning for the next meeting, the RI professional needs to take into consideration the members who contribute to the meeting, their voting habits and the outcome.

The summaries and profiles are valuable in tracking regulatory trends, and aid in planning for the company's upcoming Advisory Committee Meetings.

### Compliance and Inspection Profiles

These tools allow the RI professional to search for specific GMP, GLP or GCP compliance issues by reviewer name, compliance issue, etc., by including in their database (US-centric examples given below):
- Establishment Inspection Reports (EIR)
- Compliance letters (Warning Letters, Untitled Letters)
- Notice of Initiation of Disqualification Proceedings and Opportunity to Explain (NIDPOE)
- Notice of Opportunity for Hearing (NOOH) Letters
- FDA Form 483s
- compliance manuals
- inspection guides
- inspector profiles

### Other Add-On Services Offered:
- disease profile summaries
- comparison of competitive products
- reviewer profiles
- patent information

## Document Formats

Regulatory databases present their information in different formats, including: XML, PDF, HTML, SharePoint and MS Access. The document format and presentation are driven by the software type used to create, store and maintain the documents. Most document formats allow copying and pasting sections of the regulations into other documents.

### XML

XML stands for Extensible Markup Language, a computer language that makes information "self-describing" to the computer by explicitly stating what each significant structure is, such as a table of contents, section header, footer, etc. Hyperlinks allow the user to "jump" to the referenced document by clicking on them. Hyperlinks stand out in a document because they are a different color than the surrounding text, such as red or blue. Most regulatory agencies are moving toward accepting documents using either XML or PDF files. Documents translated into XML look like straight text unless formatting has been incorporated into the document.

### PDF

Some databases use Portable Document Format (PDF) with embedded hyperlinks. The original documents are scanned or converted into PDF and hyperlinks embedded. Once a file has been made into a PDF document, it looks like the original document, but it cannot be modified unless the user has Adobe Acrobat Writer® software and the document remains "unlocked."

**Table 3-5. Other Regulatory Information Databases**

| Provider | Contact Information | Product Benefits |
|---|---|---|
| Pharmaceutical Regulatory Services Inc. (PRS Inc.) | https://grid.pharmregservices.com/login/auth | • GRID™ (Global Regulatory Intelligence Database)—an online database of preapproval and postapproval pharmacovigilance requirements for drugs and biologics in 75+ countries |
| Thomson Reuters Accelus Regulatory Intelligence | http://accelus.thomsonreuters.com/products/accelus-regulatory-intelligence | • database for Governance, Risk and Compliance (GRC) management—offers a solution to track and analyze the regulatory changes that may impact an organization's exposure to operational, regulatory and business risk |

### HTML

Hypertext Markup Language (HTML) is the primary language of the Internet. HTML, like XML, is a language for representing documents that describes the relationship between a document's content and its format. Most documents output in this format, like XML, look like text documents (and unlike the original documents) unless special formats are applied to them.

The fastest way to search for data is using a platform that leverages XML and metadata. However, not all databases leverage this technology, which can make accessing the data slower.

## Quality Assurance

All services conduct quality checks to ensure the documents included in the databases are verified against the source documentation, so what is read in the database is, in fact, what the original document contained and is current.

## Other Strategic Regulatory Intelligence Databases

A lot of other databases are fabulous intelligence tools for strategy development, but those are covered in Chapter 12.

## Conclusion

As the need to monitor more information on a global basis increases and companies are doing more with fewer resources, RI professionals will need information to come to them already surveyed, analyzed and summarized so they can act immediately and integrate the information into their company's practices. Therefore, companies will need more from RI databases than they currently provide, such as summaries of new guidance documents, FDA reviews, "hot topics," proposed new legislation or updates to regulations; these databases also need to go further, analyzing these new items, including their potential impact on a program.

RI databases are valuable tools that no RI professional should be without, and it is expected that as the RI function grows and the need to develop global strategies increases, they will continue to add additional functionality to only increase their value. The difference in time saved and projects accomplished using these databases is similar to the difference between approval and refuse to file.

The right RI tool will depend on the needs of the organization. It is recommended that an organization thoroughly assess its business needs to identify the right tool.

# CHAPTER 4

# Regulatory Research

## What is regulatory research?

Regulatory research and the process of creating intelligence usually begin with a question: a question at a team meeting, passing in the hallway, at an Advisory Committee Meeting or after reading a publication. The requestor wants to know why, what, who, where and how regulatory can help answer the burning development question or "what if" ponderings he or she has at the moment. Drug development teams look to regulatory not only to interface with health authorities and frame submissions to meet regulator needs but, most importantly, to answer all the questions that crop up during development and to understand what the agency needs from the development process to approve a marketing application. The regulatory professional does not have to answer a question right at the meeting or at the water cooler; he or she is allowed to say, "I will get back to you." No one can be expected to know everything; true intelligence is knowing where to find something.

## An Overview of the Research Process

First, the RI professional needs a task, project or well-defined question in hand and

an idea of where to find the information (which is half the battle). Next, he or she should determine the approximate number of hours it will take to fulfill the task, project or question at hand and who the audience is, as this will dictate not only the form but the length of the response.

Subsequently, the RI professional needs to do the research, develop a response, document the response and provide it to the requester or team. Finally, the document should be filed in a logical place, since this information inevitably will need to be revisited, revised or re-used at some later time. Following is a step-by-step approach to conducting research.

## Typical Topics of Research

The types of questions asked will depend on the level of experience of individual team members or company employees, and the sophistication of the question grows with their experience. If the RI professional is stumped on where to start or even how to frame the context of the question, this is a nice time to call an RI colleague to get ideas and provide a starting place.

Typical RI topics for research include:
- clinical—indications, pathways, endpoint, development issues

- chemistry, manufacturing and controls (CMC), quality or inspection outcome issues
- Good Pharmaceutical Practice (GXP) trends
- pending legislation and recently passed legislation
- strategy, pathway development, including the use of past precedents
- labeling claims
- division or Advisory Committee profiles
- hot topics

This list is not exhaustive, as research will span all aspects of product development, and the extent of the questions can vary. Some are simple, such as, "What is an NDC number?" or more technically challenging, "What is the required number for a transdermal patch validation batch?" Or still more complex, "When will the Advanced Tissue Directive be adopted?" or "Is this potential product regulated as a drug or device?"

And of course, the question, "How can I get this specific compound approved (or how was a competitor's product approved) on a global basis?" would require a complete strategic analysis of the compound from Investigational New Drug application (IND) to New Drug Application (NDA); this is a very broad and multifaceted question.

### Tip

Never underestimate the power of Google to help provide the answer or a lead.

## Understanding the Question at Hand

Since regulatory information usually is not found in one location, the RI professional needs to have numerous sleuthing techniques in his or her armamentarium to be able to address the scope and breadth of questions posed. For each question put

forth, there are numerous sources to use when beginning the search. Information provided by the requestor will help refine and define those sources that will be needed:
- the question to be answered or document to be created (such as a development plan or strategy, clinical trial overview, pipeline analysis, presentation, how to initiate a clinical trial, etc.)
- assumptions or specifications about the product in question
- timeline

## Refining the Question

When someone says, "Give me everything on Crohn's disease," it can be interpreted as a request for a complete therapeutic overview, competitor pipeline analysis and development plan. However, if the RI professional asks for clarification, he or she might learn the requestor really wants the labels for all available drugs currently used to treat Crohn's disease. Without asking for clarification, the RI professional would not know that the information request was minimal compared to the weeks that it would take to review, research and put together a development plan. Asking for clarification does not have to be confrontational; it can be as simple as repeating back the question or mirroring with a spin on what might be requested, such as, "Just to reiterate, you asking for a complete development plan for the disease, including other drugs in development, their status, endpoints being used and the regulatory pathway used by currently approved drugs." Doing this allows the requester to think about what he or she really wants or needs and provide more detailed feedback. The RI professional also should consider the requester's background—does he or she need a full picture of all internal impacts to the full team or just as it relates to CMC, clinical, etc.

**Figure 4-1. Sample Research Checklist**

| CLINICAL CHECKLIST | |
|---|---|
| *Question:* | |
| **Key Search Terms:** | |
| | |
| | |
| | |
| | |

| SOURCES | |
|---|---|
| **Source** | **Notes** |
| ❑ FDA Website www.fda.gov | |
| ❑ Drugs@FDA http://www.accessdata.fda.gov/scripts/ cder/drugsatfda/index.cfm | |
| ❑ EMA Website http://www.ema.europa.eu/ema/index. jsp?curl=/pages/home/Home_Page. jsp&jsenabled=true | |
| ❑ Health Canada Website www.hc-sc.gc.ca/dhp-mps/index-eng.php | |
| ❑ DIAhome.org | |
| ❑ RAPS.org | |
| ❑ Medline http://www.ncbi.nlm.nih.gov/pubmed/ | |
| ❑ Clinicaltrials.gov | |
| ❑ ACRPnet.org | |
| ❑ http://www.appliedclinicaltrialsonline. com/ | |
| ❑ GCP Journal http://www.pjbpubs.com/cms. asp?pageid=684 | |

## Defining Key Search Terms

Once the question or topic is defined, the RI professional can move forward and break the question down into key words or concepts such as:

- transdermal patch validation batch
- number of 505(b)(2) applications done to date for analgesics or a particular FDA division (key words: 505(b)(2) and analgesics or name of division)
- how to file a 505(b)(2) and can it be done for this product (key words: 505(b)(2) and class of compound)
- will an application be a 505(b)(2) or 505(b)(1); differences and similarities in application types (key words: 505(b)(2), 505(b)(1), how to file an NDA, NDA)

**Figure 4-2. Regulatory Research Data Collection/Presentation Format**

| REGULATORY RESEARCH | |
|---|---|
| **Type:**<br>**Device:** | **Drug:** |
| **Indication:** | **Claimed effect:** |
| **Principal Mechanism of Action: Pharmacologic** | |
| *Question:* | |
| **SUMMARY** | |
| *Background and Definitions* | |
| • | |
| *Assumptions* | |
| • | |
| *Strategic Advice* | |
| • | |
| *Recommendation* | |
| • | |
| References:<br>1<br><br>2<br><br>3 | |

*Note: This form can be used and modified as needed for the question asked and technology involved.*

- how to file a Canadian Clinical Trial Application (CTA) (key words: Canadian CTA, Health Canada Clinical Trial Application)
- International Nonproprietary Name (INN), application (key words: INN process)
- how many products received Fast Track designation, Priority Review and received orphan designation; US, EU, Japan and Australia; terminology differences in accelerated approval pathways (key words: Fast Track US, Fast Track Japan, Fast Track EU, etc.)

When the key terms are determined, the RI professional can start pulling up the needed websites, starting with specific websites or a general "Google" search.

Key terms should be used as they would be for a Medline search.

- if the subject is complex, it should be broken down initially into a few key words
- a "search within results" will further refine the topic if too many "hits" are returned, or more key words can be added to constrict search
- a search for terms on screen (control f) will find terms not highlighted in information
- the RI professional should take the time to drill down into documents

It always helps if the RI professional tracks key terms and has a trail that can be retraced if needed and can serve as a reminder of where not to return. Some regulatory submissions (e.g., Development Safety Update Report or orphan drug application) actually need to include all key terms searched, so this documentation might be invaluable to the end user.

**Figure 4-1** provides a sample checklist for conducting clinical searches. Checklists can be made for regulatory, general, CMC, clinical and nonclinical to help guide searches and track key terms.

## Typical Locations to Start the Search

Finding regulatory information usually is not a one-stop shopping trip. The RI professional needs to be able to address the scope and breadth of questions posed, particularly in a small company or as an independent consultant. For each question posed, there are numerous sources to begin the search, including the following:

- online professional and scientific article subscriptions
- regulatory agency sites
- previous regulatory submissions (internal to the company)
- competitors' previous submissions (summary basis of approvals (SBAs), 510(k)s, Premarket Approval Applications (PMAs) and European Public Assessment Reports (EPARs))
- competitors' marketing literature
- RI databases
- email alerts
- educational conferences
- regulatory reference and information sites
- local chapter meetings of various organizations
- colleagues

### Tip

It is okay to use Wikipedia as a place to start, but the RI professional should not copy and paste information from it; go to the source to get the information (verify the information; FDA will).

- business intelligence websites and databases
- Advisory Committee Meeting minutes
- books
- consultants

## How to Conduct the Search and Compile Information

To compile research and intelligence, the author uses the format in **Figure 4-2** as a starting point, a way to store data and, for some projects, as the presentation format. RI professionals should follow these step-by-step instructions for transforming research and information into intelligence.

1. Create a short list of key terms that will be used in conducting the search; this list can be expanded based on research results.
2. Research the topic and cull all pertinent information about the research topic from resources. They also should do a general search, including a wide variety of sources and refining the key terms as needed. All these results, usually PDFs, should be placed in a folder and all sites visited captured as hyperlinks in the reference section because someone will always want to verify the information provided.
3. Read pertinent information about the research topic.
4. Write a summary of each piece of information after reading it. Add these to appropriate sections in the research review template (such as Background and Definitions)—this will help frame the search and the questions.
5. Analyze the findings in relation to the initial question. Analyzing the findings will allow more questions to arise.
6. Allow additional questions to arise, based on the analysis. Additional questions will provide a wider perspective of the information and the parameters

**Graphic 4-1. Overview of Regulatory Research**

The question (which may be ambiguous) being asked should be defined. This can be divided into subsections if there are several components to the question or strategy.

- Background information should be defined, including:
  - definitions (to provide clarification to team members)
  - concepts used
  - regulations or guidelines
  - succinct summarization of background information (including above) pertinent to the question
- Assumptions—sometimes when working with limited information, the RI professional needs to make assumptions, and this is a good way to capture them. If the assumptions change, the recommendations and the strategy can be adapted.
- Strategic advice—after careful review of the research and question, the answer can take a variety of approaches, based on the question asked, such as:
  - impact on the current program
  - proposal to incorporate the question asked in the drug development program
  - steps to mitigate risk to the current program
  - next steps to take in the development program
  - how to begin a development program
- Recommendations—the practical steps or "action items" to implement the strategy
- References—will be organized and documented and can be appended if necessary and can include:
  - pertinent regulations and guidance documents
  - websites
  - articles or other publications

that need to be considered when formulating a solid response. Additional questions also might bring about the need for additional searches and different key terms.

7. Write up an analysis. The RI professional should pull together all the pieces of information and analyze how they fit and impact one another and then develop recommendations, provide strategic advice (both are not always necessary) or explain how it impacts the current program. The background and definitions should be succinct, and all assumptions about the product should be captured.

8. Expert Review. Not everything needs an expert review, but sometimes, for clinical development pathways or for commenting, external experts should review the documents before they are distributed to the team or outside the company.

9. Make recommendations or give strategic advice. This is where the RI professional's regulatory expertise can shine, by making recommendations on the material compiled and analyzed. Some teams want to debate all the findings, and that is fine, but as a first step, the RI professional should go in with a position he or she can support. Other teams rely on the RI professional to be the expert and will accept his or her recommendations without debate; it all depends on company culture.

10. How does the RI professional know when the search is done? The search is over when the primary question has been answered, and no more pertinent secondary questions arise that cannot be answered or dismissed.

11. Format the findings for the audience. Once the information has been summarized, the RI professional will need to put it in a standard format to integrate the

current position and recent information to deliver information to the target audience.

12. Deliver the information to the target audience via the medium of their choice.

13. Archive and document the work. The RI professional should collect all his or her back-up and put it together in one folder or document and store it on an RI drive under the question name for posterity, or post on a shared drive for all to review.

## What does the research output look like?

The answer depends on who the audience members are and their level in the company, which, in turn, will dictate the amount of information that should be provided to the requestor.

## Let Form Follow Information Function

When transforming information into intelligence, there is no set way to display regulatory output. The output should define the format and most effective presentation to the end user. RI allows the regulatory professional to be creative in sleuthing techniques and data presentation. However, once a way to present information is established, it is good if it stays consistent so people know what to expect and where to look for the requested information. **Figure 4-3** provides an example of output.

## Know the Audience

Not only does the question or intelligence dictate the format, so does the ultimate audience. When the RI professional is planning the final product format, he or she needs to consider how the information will affect or impact the target audience, team or strategy. A comparison of the audience and level of detail needed for the same project presented to a variety

of personnel types and levels within the company are discussed below.

## Recipient Level

### Management (VP or "C" Level)

The RI professional should present a succinct overview of three to five slides with the same number of bullet points per slide and always include:

- the problem
- the impact to the company (short term and long term, including fiscal impact)
- proposed resolution to the problem and management buy-in
- cost (if applicable)

Tip: The RI professional should never go to management with a problem without at least a proposed solution—they want well thought-out solutions to problems, not just issues.

### Core Team/Product Development Team

Construct a presentation of five to 20 slides in length, providing:

- the question
- background of why the question is important to the team
- high-level summary (that is or can be presented to the "C" team, because management probably will elevate it, if needed)
- details of the development plan or question addressed
- conclusion
- impact on the company
- proposed solution and discussion

### Tip

A picture is worth a thousand words, so, for management presentations, the information can be put in a graphics presentation, such as the popular "Funnel" design used for showing the Clinical Development Competitive landscapes.

**Figure 4-3. Sample Regulatory Research Output**

| REGULATORY STRATEGY | |
|---|---|
| **Type**: Drug/Device combination | **Drug:** Hydromorphone hydrochloride |
| | **Device:** Transdermal patch with electrical components |
| **Indication**: Management of chronic pain | **Claimed effect (proposed)**: Management of moderate to severe chronic pain due to malignant conditions |
| **Principal Mechanism of Action: Pharmacologic** | |
| *Question: Will this drug/device be regulated as a drug or device or combination product in Canada?* | |
| **SUMMARY** | |
| *Background and Definitions* | |
| • Health Canada defines a combination product as "a therapeutic product that combines a drug component and a device component, such that the distinctive nature of the drug component and device component is integrated in a singular product." Within this definition, "drug" refers to both drug and biologic products. | |
| • Where the principal mechanism of action by which the claimed effect or purpose is achieved by **pharmacological**, immunological, or metabolic means, the combination product will be subject to the *Food and Drug Regulations*, unless that action occurs *in vitro*, without reintroducing a modified cellular substance to the patient, in which case the product will be subject to the *Medical Devices Regulations*.[1] | |
| • **Pharmacological** is understood as an interaction between the molecules of the substance in question and a cellular constituent, usually referred to as a receptor, which either results in a direct response, or which blocks the response to another agent and, for the purposes of this policy, includes anti-infective activity.[2] | |
| • The Combination Product policy does not apply to combinations of drugs and medical devices where the drug component and the device component can be used separately (e.g. products sold together in procedure packages and trays). The *Food and Drug Regulations* shall apply to the drug component of such a product and the *Medical Devices Regulations* shall apply to the device component.[2] | |
| *Assumptions* | |
| • Put in assumptions about drug and device | |
| *Strategic Advice* | |
| • The primary mechanism of action is due to the pharmacological means, therefore, in Canada, this will be regulated as a drug combination product and subject to the *Food and Drug Regulations*. | |
| *Recommendation* | |
| • Example: File a Clinical Trials Application for a drug | |
| References: | 1  Drug and Medical Device Combination Product Decisions, 7 June 1999 |
| | 2  Drug/Medical Device Combination Products, 12 June 1997, revised May 1999 |

| REGULATORY STRATEGY | |
|---|---|
| **Type**: Drug | **Drug:** Betamethasone valerate 0.1% |
| | **Device:** topical foam |
| **Indication:** Corticosteroid-responsive dermatoses | **Claimed effect (proposed)**: Relief of inflammatory and pruritic manifestations of corticosteroid-responsive dermatoses of the scalp |
| **Principal Mechanism of Action: Pharmacologic** | |
| *Question: Can a 505(b)(2) NDA be filed or will a traditional 505(b)(1) NDA be required?* | |
| **SUMMARY** | |

*Background and Definitions*

- *505(b)(2) Application* means an application submitted under section 505(b)(1) of the act for a drug for which the investigations described in section 505(b)(1)(A) of the act and relied upon by the applicant for approval of the application were not conducted by or for the applicant and for which the applicant has not obtained a right of reference or use from the person by or for whom the investigations were conducted.[1]

- *Right of reference or use* means the authority to rely upon, and otherwise use, an investigation for the purpose of obtaining approval of an application, including the ability to make available the underlying raw data from the investigation for FDA audit, if necessary.[1]

Section 505 of the Act describes three types of new drug applications:
- an application that contains full reports of investigations of safety and effectiveness (section 505(b)(1));
- (2) an application that contains full reports of investigations of safety and effectiveness but where at least some of the information required for approval comes from studies not conducted by or for the applicant and for which the applicant has not obtained a right of reference (section 505(b)(2)); and
- (3) an application that contains information to show that the proposed product is identical in active ingredient, dosage form, strength, route of administration, labeling, quality, performance characteristics, and intended use, among other things, to a previously approved product (section 505(j)). Note that a supplement to an application is a new drug application. [2]

- A 505(b)(2) application can rely on
  - *Published literature*
  - *The Agency's finding of safety and effectiveness for an approved drug*[2]

What kind of application can be submitted as a 505(b)(2) application?
  - *New chemical entity (NCE)/new molecular entity (NME)*
  - *Changes to previously approved drugs*[2]

What Are Some Examples Of 505(B)(2) Applications?
  - *Dosage form*
  - *Strength*
  - *Route of administration*
  - *Formulation*
  - *Dosing regimen*
  - *Active ingredient*
  - *Indication*[2]

*Assumptions*

- This is a new dosage form and indication for a previously approved drug
- New dosage form acts like innovator lotion when applied
- Refer to nonclinical and safety data of innovator drug
- Refer to published literature

*Strategic Advice*

- Minimal clinical data will be needed to support a marketing application
- A bridging study needs to be conducted comparing new dosage form and marketed product(s).
- Hold a meeting with the FDA to present development plan

*Recommendation*

- Conduct a clinical "bridging" study
- File a 505 (b)(2) application for new indication based on innovator's NDA with new clinical data to support indication and new dosage form

| References: | 1 | 21 CFR §314.3–Definitions |
|---|---|---|
| | 2 | Guidance for Industry, Applications Covered by Section 505(b)(2), 1999 |
| | 3 | 21 CFR §314.54 Procedure for submission of an application requiring investigations for approval of a new indication for or other change from, a listed drug |
| | 4 | Innovator NDAs: 16-322 for cream 0.1% and 0.01%<br>16-740 for ointment 0.1%<br>16-932 for lotion 0.1% |

### Company Wide (SharePoint or Intranet Site)

The front page of the regulatory research or overview should be included. Support documents are available on request, so outdated documents will not be used when the research is reviewed by members outside regulatory.

### Department-Specific Regulatory Research

A copy of the regulatory research format should be given to the requester, typically without all the backup, but a list of hyperlinked references should be included. Typically, other departments want synthesized information with all the backup details available if they want to look at them.

### Regulatory

The RI professional should use the regulatory research format and make all backup documents available.

### Document, Document, Document

Once the research is done, presented and distributed, what does the RI professional do with it? It often is easier after a great deal of work has been done to not finalize the documentation but to move on to another time-sensitive project. RI professionals should be forewarned that, although management may gear up for one project and then drop it like a hot potato to move on to another project, they usually revisit it within a year's time. So, if the work is documented, it only will need to be revised in a year's time to ensure it is still current.

Suggestions for storing RI include:
- keep a hard copy in a department filing cabinet
- scan it and put it on an electronic shared drive
- scan it and include it in an RI database or department intranet site

CHAPTER 5

# Monitoring and Surveillance

## Surveillance as Part of the Regulatory Toolbox

Regulatory is expected to know the regulatory landscape, when it changes and the impact on the team, the company or product being developed. If changes in the regulatory landscape occur without regulatory reporting the change (or the impact on the team), regulatory can lose credibility and potentially delay a product reaching the market, costing the company millions of dollars.

Some regulatory professionals do not start the day with the *Federal Register* or FDA (or other health authority) news feeds, daily newsletters, etc. By doing this, they are leaving themselves open to being scooped by other departments that do start their day with these items or, worse yet, not being informed or current. A regulatory professional's job is to keep abreast of any changes and keep current; however, the extent and depth to which the RI professional tracks the changing landscape will depend on the company size and culture, products and interest in the topic. No matter the size, the RI professional's day should start with reviewing the health authority of choice's daily feeds, at minimum.

## What is surveillance?

Also called monitoring (the terms are used interchangeably), surveillance is the worldwide monitoring of regulatory information to look for changes in the regulatory landscape or for only one country if that is what the RI professional is covering. For what kind of changes should the RI professional be looking?

- changes in laws, regulations, directives, guidance documents, etc.
- upcoming laws, regulations, directives, guidance documents, etc.
- changes in agency policy, organization, etc.
- compliance trends, Warning Letters issued or inspection findings
- approvals, impact or risks to approval (due to new regulations, advisory committee meeting outcomes, articles, recent marketing application rejections, new guidance documents, etc.)

Typically, surveillance is conducted either periodically or an ongoing basis.

Periodic surveillance is conducted only when a question arises, so surveillance is conducted at the time of research and review of the topic at hand, rather than looking at ongoing changes in the landscape. This normally is done because a company is small, and the available resources for continual surveillance might be limited. A disadvantage of periodic surveillance is that topics of interest might be missed, depending on timeframes between surveillance intervals.

With ongoing surveillance, issues tend not to be missed, and companies keep abreast of them. A database or other software tool usually is used to conduct continual surveillance of health authority websites and other information of interest.

For a small company, monitoring and review of its results can be conducted on a weekly basis, but most large companies do this on a daily basis from either their headquarters or affiliates.

Again, at minimum, an RI professional should read the US *Federal Register* or its equivalent in different countries to keep abreast of regulatory changes.

## What are typical surveillance topics?

The answer to this question depends on the company and how the RI department is organized. For example, an analyst might be interested only in changes in clinical trial regulations, how to conduct clinical trials or clinical trial requirements in the 90 countries that have regulatory systems. This analyst would be tracking health authority websites for any changes in legislation, regulations, directives or guidances as they pertain to clinical trials. This analyst also would look at professional publications and trade journals for articles concerning upcoming changes. In addition, the analyst would attend professional meetings and talks discussing changes in the clinical trials environment in the countries being monitored, to thoroughly assess the landscape.

Other topics for monitoring can include:
- modifications to existing laws, regulations, directives and guidance documents
- changes in agency structure
- nonclinical studies (pharmacology, pharmacokinetics, pharmacodynamics, toxicology, immunogenicity, genotoxicity, etc.)
- how to file a marketing application
- how to maintain a marketing application
- manufacturing requirements, including specific dosage forms
- stability requirements, including different materials and dosage forms
- Good Manufacturing Practices (GMPs), Good Clinical Practice (GCP), Good Laboratory Practice (GLP) or any Good (anything) Practice (GXP)
- any other topics important to the company to support product development

## Where to Start

Where does the RI professional tasked with conducting surveillance for a region or the whole globe start? The professional needs to have tools in his or her armamentarium to manage, organize and categorize project-specific information for retrieval and review, while avoiding information overload. And of course, the professional's toolbox and ability to accurately capture information all depends on his or her experience, the budget and company size.

## How to Monitor the Landscape

The first step prior to conducting monitoring needs to be agreement on what the RI professional actually will monitor.
- Are only regulatory agencies being monitored? If only regulatory agencies, the drug, device or biologics divisions or all of them?
- Which countries are included in the monitoring?
- Is the RI professional responsible for all countries or is this a shared or regional responsibility (for larger companies)?
- What specific disciplines will be monitored, such as GLP, GCP, GMP, clinical trial start up,

marketing application requirements, etc.?

- Are there any specific product approvals or withdrawals that should be monitored?
- Are there specific guidance documents or regulations that should be monitored?
- Are there any specific companies the RI professional should monitor?

Once these questions are answered, the regulatory professional needs to think about the key terms to use when searching; timing and frequency of searches; and the tools, websites and budget needed to conduct surveillance.

## Surveillance Intervals: Periodic

The budget and company size also will determine how frequently surveillance can be conducted. Small companies have limited resources and may not understand how a lack of surveillance can impact them. In some cases, the impact can be so severe that it can affect their marketing application approvability. Therefore, they should outsource this function, so key information is not missed. For a small company, surveillance typically is conducted:

- when a question comes up, usually around a competitor approval or something someone heard from a colleague at a meeting the person wants investigated further
- when the development team wants to understand the regulatory landscape or risks to a particular product approval

## Surveillance Intervals: Ongoing

If a consulting firm, regulatory intelligence database or other software is employed to conduct daily surveillance, thus reducing the personnel dedicated to this effort, issues critical to the company tend not to get missed (someone does need to review the daily surveillance results and decide whether it is actionable).

## Small Company Surveillance

In small companies, RI is more reactive, since small companies typically do not have the resources to be proactive, which leaves them at a competitive disadvantage:

- fewer resources than a medium or large company
- person conducting surveillance might not have the same sharpened tool kit for conducting surveillance as someone who performs this on a daily basis
- dependent on free email alerts and newsletters to learn about upcoming changes (e.g., FDA news feeds and the Food and Drug Law Institute's *FDLI SmartBrief*)
- dependent on colleagues and a developed network to inform the company about upcoming changes (only as good as network colleagues)
- regulatory professionals visit available international websites and look for "What's New" section to find out about new legislation (which can be in a non-native language)

## Large Company Surveillance

Large companies have RI functions that can survey the global landscape on a daily basis, so issues that affect product approvability are not missed and can be incorporated into the product strategy and planning. They also have regional offices to provide up-to-date changes for a country or region that can feed into a larger monitoring program.

## Surveillance Tools: Free

### Regulatory Agency Feeds

For a US-based company, the easiest way for RI professionals to keep informed is to monitor the daily *Federal Register* (https://www.federalregister.gov/agencies/food-and-drug-administration). If an RI professional subscribes to the site, he or she will receive daily emails about new regulations, comment periods, meetings and other items. It should be a ritual to read the email first thing in the morning; this is the cheapest way to conduct surveillance and keep abreast of the changes in the US regulatory landscape. The RI professional also should sign up for FDA's feeds that provide notices of drug approvals, withdrawals, meetings and new guidance documents.

- Email feeds (www.fda.gov/ AboutFDA/ContactFDA/ StayInformed/GetEmailUpdates/ default.htm)
- RSS Feeds: www.fda.gov/ AboutFDA/ContactFDA/ StayInformed/RSSFeeds/default. htm

Recent EMA news can be found at www.ema.europa.eu/ema/index. jsp?curl=pages/home/Home_Page. jsp&mid, and the RI professional can subscribe to the EMA RSS feeds at www.ema.europa.eu/ema/ index.jsp?curl=pages/news_ and_events/landing/rss_feed. jsp&mid=WC0b01ac058007c0e8

Other large health authorities also have RSS feeds (see below for more details), "What's new" sites and email alerts, although the languages used vary by country. For a complete listing of all health authority websites, please see www. regulatorium.com/intelligence-links.html.

## Publications

The next level of surveillance is the *FDLI SmartBrief*, which provides a summary of news in the US drug, device, biologic and dietary supplement markets. Members of RAPS or DIA also may subscribe to daily or weekly newsletters that are very helpful. Other publications that provide in-depth analysis typically are by subscription only.

## Blogs and News Sites

It is easy to get inundated with information, so the RI professional should choose daily or weekly visits carefully. Sometimes an RI professional only look at blogs when it is a topic related to research he or she is conducting. Blogs can be fantastic in provide timely analysis of a recently issued guidance, pressing issues, a regulatory trend or a hot topic. Caution should be exercised when reviewing articles and blogs; the information presented might not be complete, and the viewpoint may be biased, so it is advisable to read many perspectives to understand the whole picture. Blogs of choice include:

- FDA Voice (blogs.fda.gov)
- LinkedIn groups
- blog.pharmexec.com
- www.fdalawblog.net/
- www.eyeonfda.com
- www.fiercebiotech.com
- www.fiercepharma.com
- www.pharmalot.com

## Alert Services

These services troll the Internet and find the content the RI professional is seeking, especially if it is a "hot topic," competitor information, specific therapeutic area drug launches or developing regulation. Is there a downside? Issues include information overload, sites not screened for content and vulnerability to computer viruses. Currently, there is no better way to keep up with developing trends or stories.

*RSS Feeds (Rich Site Summary or Really Simple Syndication)*
RSS is an alert service that uses XML-based (looks like plain text) feeds to publish frequently updated information such as blog entries, news headlines, audio and video. An RSS feed includes full or summarized text and metadata. Once users subscribe to a website, RSS removes the need for them to manually check it. Instead, their browsers constantly monitor the site and inform the user of any updates via email. Is there a downside? Besides information overload, users have to individually subscribe to each website's RSS feed and install a reader. Subscribing involves clicking on the orange symbol on all websites of interest. For a starter list of feeds to follow, please see "Using RSS Feeds as a Regulatory Intelligence Tool: The Feeds you Need to Follow" in *Regulatory Focus* July 2013.

*Google Alerts (www.google.com/alerts)*
Google Alerts is a way to set up email alerts anytime new information is uploaded to the web about a topic, product or company. This is a way to be alerted to any changes, but the frequency sometimes can be overwhelming, so RI professionals need to maintain a monitoring list to get relevant information. Google Alerts has gotten some bad press as of late due to slowness in delivering information, so a few competitors have cropped up, namely Mention and Talk Walker Alerts.

*Mention (en.mention.net)*
Mention is similar to Google Alerts. RI professionals can track up to 500 results per month for up to three keywords for free (more key words results in a monthly fee). Mention pulls results in 42 languages from Facebook, Twitter, news sites, blogs, forums and other websites, and includes image and video results as well. Like Google Alerts, it is possible to receive updates through email on a daily or weekly basis, or solely through the Mention dashboard.

*TalkWalker Alerts (www.talkwalker.com/alerts)*
Just like Google Alerts, Talkwalker Alerts is an easy and free alerting service that provides email updates of the latest relevant mentions on the web directly to the user's email box or RSS feed reader. They monitor various online and social media sources such as blogs, news, forums and social networks, and the RI professional can specify language, the kind of media to be monitored, key terms, the number of results and frequency of delivery.

### Google Translate

According to international shipping company Federal Express, there are 220 countries in the world, and the United Nations (UN) recognizes 193. Of those 193, about 90 have regulatory systems. There are between 6,800 and 6,900 languages in the world. The UN has six official languages used in meetings: Arabic, Chinese, English, French, Russian and Spanish.

In monitoring global regulatory affairs, regulatory professionals often want to read the source document but face a language barrier. Google Translate (translate.google.com) is a free service that provides instant translations of website content or individual documents—so once a document has been downloaded during surveillance efforts, Google Translate can help to some extent. The service supports 58 different languages and is a fantastic tool for getting the gist of the regulatory requirements. Google Translate is great at translating most South American and Western and Eastern European languages, although Middle Eastern and Asian language translations are not as reliable. Also, when a document has a lot of graphics or tables, it sometimes does not translate into intelligible information.

If the regulatory professional is relying on a document as the basis of regulatory strategy, intelligence or compliance, Google Translate can in no way replace a professional translation, back translation and certification process, but it can help in deciding which documents may need a full translation. Both Tarius and IDRAC/Cortellis offer translations of documents contained in their databases.

## Surveillance Tools: Fee

If the company has an RI budget and supports a more extensive surveillance program, the tools below can help more accurately capture what is happening in the world of regulatory intelligence.

### Copernic Tracker http://www.copernic.com/en/products/tracker/)

Copernic Tracker is an inexpensive surveillance tool that automatically looks for new content on web pages (programmed into the software by the RI professional) as often as desired. When a change is detected, the tracking software will send an email, including a copy of the web page with the changes highlighted. Copernic Tracker will help track:
- online forums and social media
- news sites

- product updates
- competitors' websites

### Publications

Publications are a way to follow regulatory trends, hot topics and compliance and inspection issues. Most require an annual subscription and are available online. Please see www.regulatorium.com/intelligence-links.html for a complete and up-to-date listing of recommended publications. If Copernic Tracker or RSS feeds are used for publication sites, areas of interest will be delivered to the RI professional's inbox.

### Professional Association Meetings

This is where up-to-date information will be found on forthcoming changes in the regulatory arena as health authorities present upcoming changes and programs, and industry experts discuss how they are handling new or pending legislation. While there are a number of conferences, the annual RAPS and DIA meetings are always the best places to learn new information. To ensure intelligence gained at meetings is shared and made actionable, the RI professional should:

- Identify the types of information expected to be gathered at the meeting and how it will be used (this can help justify the expense of attending).
- Identify and delegate company representatives who have the subject matter expertise to understand and interpret not only the expected information but also the unexpected information gleaned.
- Prior to the meeting, hold an internal briefing session for participants that defines general and specific information they should capture at the meeting through the creation of a standardized electronic document for capturing session/meeting intelligence, and ask the participants to obtain an electronic copy of the presentation whenever possible. A

standardized format allows direct downloading into a shared RI database or document sharing database or site.
- After the meeting ends, the new intelligence should be posted to the database or shared site, and for the really hot topics, a "lessons learned" lunchtime event should be scheduled for all interested participants.

### Advisory Committee Meetings

This is the best surveillance tool for competitive intelligence if the RI professional can attend in person to see the information presented, and hear the agency's questions and the company's responses. If unable to attend the meeting, the RI professional should read the meeting package posted by FDA, review the FDALive.com DVD or, if the company subscribes to IDRAC's ADComm Bulletin or Tarius' SAC Tracker, read the condensed and summarized information available a few hours after the meeting.

### RI Databases

The best solution is one delivered by RI database providers. Tailored newsletters can be delivered on a daily or weekly basis that list all newly published documents across the RI professional's selection of countries and areas of interest in a single report.

It also is possible to set up 'alerts,' which will notify the professional immediately when new documents matching the search criteria are published.

## What are the Outcomes of Surveillance?

There must be a purpose for monitoring websites and publications and a reason to spend the time and resources required for this activity. Some outcomes of surveillance include:

- analyzing new information for its impact on the current program or product and determining whether anything new needs to be implemented to accommodate this new information

- summarizing the information for team members and allowing them to determine the impact on the company and program
- no action required after review of information

## How to Process Incoming Surveillance Data

When a company first sets up a surveillance program, the amount of data coming in can be overwhelming until filters have been applied or processes and personnel put in place to deal with the onslaught of data. Below is an example of handling incoming data:

- Data Received: Decision Point— Are the data applicable to the company? If so, priority for the review and analysis should be assigned (urgent, project related, as time permits, etc.) and filed in the appropriate folder, and the person doing analysis should be contacted. If they are not pertinent, discard them or keep in a topic-defined folder for later review.
- Write a summary of each piece of information.
- Analyze the findings in relation to the current process, procedure or research question.
- Write up the analysis.
- Make recommendations or give strategic advice.
- Format the findings for the intended audience and communicate them to stakeholders.
- Document and archive the work.

## Real Life Examples

- A small company did not monitor the landscape (specifically the trade journals, publications and blogs that said FDA was looking at changing the safety database requirements for Type I and II diabetes indications, or the Actos

and Avandia safety issues or Advisory Committee Meetings that followed). When it filed its marketing application, it was caught off guard when the agency said the application was not approvable due to the small safety database of 325 patients.
  - o Solution: If the company had monitored the landscape, it could have met with the agency to negotiate the old safety database number of 325 (instead of new requirements for 2,500 patients) or realized before filing the marketing application that additional trials needed to be conducted.
  - o Impact: The company could not raise the money needed to conduct the additional Phase 3 trial that was needed and, as a result, closed.
- A small company did not know ICH had issued new stability guidance and was caught off guard when FDA did not agree with its submitted stability program during the Pre-NDA Meeting (and the material had already been manufactured and put on the old stability program).
  - o Impact: 14-month delay to the marketing application filing and layoffs.
- A small company was unaware that a nonclinical guidance document was withdrawn, and its nonclinical studies were conducted according to the old guidance. The company was caught by surprise when its IND was placed on clinical hold due to the need for additional nonclinical studies.
  - o Impact: One-year clinical hold and layoffs.

**References**
"Using RSS Feeds as a Regulatory Intelligence Tool: The Feeds You Need to Follow" in RAPS Focus July 2013.

CHAPTER 6

# Drug Approvals and Past Precedents

Part of the RI professional's responsibility is keeping a finger on the pulse of the regulatory landscape in the company's predefined therapeutic area. This includes monitoring drugs on the market, research and current innovations, new drugs in development, promising drugs, classification of compounds (class of drugs), ongoing trials, investigational milestones (such as agency meetings or completing a clinical trial), orphan drug designations, accelerated or breakthrough therapy designations, safety issues, withdrawals, labeling changes and drug approvals in specific countries.

When putting together a strategy, the RI professional needs to look at all the approved drugs in the therapeutic area to summarize the landscape. Sometimes all the information can be found in one place; other times it is necessary to use many different sources to pull together the complete picture. One way to keep abreast of a therapeutic area is to review past precedents.

## What is a past precedent?

According to *Webster's Collegiate Dictionary*, a precedent is:
- an earlier occurrence of something similar
- something done or said that may serve as an example or rule to authorize or justify a subsequent act of the same or analogous kind
- a person or thing that serves as a model[1]

In the context of RI, a past precedent is everything about a drug that has been approved, including but not limited to:
- health authority websites
- health authority presentations
- previous approvals (FDA—Summary Basis of Approval (SBA) (now known as FDA Approval Packages), EMA—European Public Assessment Report (EPAR), Health Canada—Summary Basis of Decision (SBD), Therapeutic Goods Administration (TGA)—Australian Public Assessment Report (AusPAR))
- labeling
- minutes from interactions with health authorities
- Advisory Committee briefing packages and transcripts (US)
- postmarketing commitments database
- patent and exclusivity information

- Pediatric Written Requests, Pediatric Investigational Plans (PIPs) or Pediatric Study Plans (PSPs)
- Inactive Ingredients Database (US)
- clinical trial disclosure websites—World Health Organization (WHO), International Federation of Pharmaceutical Manufacturers and Associations (IFPMA), European Clinical Trials Database (EudraCT), clinicaltrials.gov, etc.
- competitor information (press releases)
- compliance issues (FDA 483s, Warning Letters, Notice of Initiation of Disqualification Proceedings and Opportunity to Explain (NIDPOE) letters, debarment, restrictions, scientific misconduct, US)
- EudraGMDP (EU database of manufacturing, import and wholesale-distribution authorizations and Good Manufacturing Practice and Good Distribution Practice certificates)

This chapter focuses on how the RI professional can review filings as they become available. The reviews are posted not to help industry, but to provide transparency of the agency's procedures and decision making for the consumer.

Note: Information should be current, which means since the implementation of ICH in 1996, so anything after 1997 should be reviewed. If a past precedent prior to 1997 is being reviewed, the RI professional must take into account changes in the nonclinical and clinical standards and the development program will need to reflect this (i.e., additional nonclinical and clinical trials will be needed to bring the filing up to current standards, so studies would need to be conducted that were not necessarily required of the innovator).

## What does a past precedent provide?

A past precedent provides a basis for what was previously allowed by the health authority or agency. The agency typically follows the same approval requirements for all drugs, unless an extraordinary circumstance exists that warrants a waiver of some requirements (accelerated approval or orphan drugs). Although FDA's divisions work with the same regulations and guidances, they also are independent in how they apply these regulations, so reading a variety of past precedents (also called SBAs or reviews) provides a sense of the division's requirements. However, international health authorities are more consistent in their requirements.

An SBA, EPAR, AusPAR or SBD is a snapshot that reflects the legislative, regulatory and scientific environment at the time of drug review and approval, which may not reflect current thinking. Therefore, reviewing past precedents might only provide a starting place and not the final destination. These summary reviews typically include information on medical or clinical analysis, chemistry, clinical pharmacology, biopharmaceutics, pharmacology, statistics, microbiology, environmental analysis, final label and approval histories (administrative documents, approval letters, correspondence).

For example, if a company is developing a Type II diabetes drug, the RI professional should look at past filings, including Actos and Avandia. The SBA on FDA's website (first review only) will give a very different perspective of what is required for a Type II diabetes drug than recent reviews of these drugs, which contain important updated safety information. Stopping there also would provide an incomplete picture without reading the trade press concerning drug safety issues and transcripts from the Advisory Committee Meetings. There is now a Risk Evaluation and Mitigation Strategy (REMS) site on the FDA website devoted to these drugs. The guidance document pertaining to Type II diabetes drugs will help round out the current drug development picture. A past precedent is part of the picture but, depending on the length of time the drug has been on the market, multiple sources of information should be considered.

**Table 6-1. Template to Collect Information for Drug Summary**

| Drug Name | |
|---|---|
| NDA # (Sponsor) | |
| Indication:<br>Mechanism of Action: | |
| Dosage Form | |
| Classification (505(b)(1), 505(b)(2), 505(j)) | |
| Number of Clinical Studies Needed for Approval | |
| Phase 1 | |
| Phase 2 | |
| Phase 3 | |
| Final Safety Database | |
| Were pediatric studies done or was a waiver requested? | |
| Nonclinical Studies | |
| Any CMC issues? | |
| How many times was the NDA submitted before the drug or biologic was approved? | |
| If rejected after the first submission, what were the reasons for the nonapproval? | |
| How long was it between the first NDA submission and final approval of the drug? | |
| What was the tone of communication with FDA? | |
| What were the proposed and final trade names? | |

## What is not in the reviews?

Commercially confidential information is redacted from all reviews, and the NDA sponsor, in the past, has let the agency know what it considers confidential. Gathering data from multiple regulatory agencies will help assemble the whole picture or reverse engineer the development program, but some information always remains confidential.

## Can precedents be retrieved prior to product approval?

It all depends, of course, which is the great regulatory answer. It depends on the internal company resources and how the company values the importance of monitoring the competitive landscape.

The short answer is no, this information is not provided until after the drug is approved by the first regulatory agency that issues publically available reviews. All IND and CTA information is kept confidential, except certain clinical trial information, until after the marketing application is approved. The long answer is yes, of course, if the RI professional is willing to hunt for the answer or has the budget to pay for pipeline tools (see Chapter 12 Strategy for more details). Prior to a drug being approved, it is possible to find:

- clinical endpoints—it is possible to get a good idea of the drug development program

**Table 6-2. Example of a Brief Summary of an Approved Drug**

| Drug Name | Sprycel™ (dasatinib) |
|---|---|
| NDA # (Sponsor) | NDA 021986 (Bristol-Myers Squibb) |
| Indication:<br>Mechanism of Action: | Chronic Myelogenous Leukemia (CML)<br>MOA: tyrosine kinase inhibitor (BCR-ABL, SRC, PDGFRB) |
| Dosage Form | Oral tablets (20mg, 50mg, 70mg) |
| Classification (505(b)(1), 505(b)(2), 505(j) | 505(b)(1) |
| Number of Clinical Studies Needed for Approval | 6 clinical studies for approval |
| Phase 1 | 1 completed, multicenter, dose-escalation PI trial supportive in the evaluation of safety and efficacy—84 patients |
| Phase 2 | 5 completed, PII trials pivotal in the evaluation of safety and efficacy—total 565 patients<br>• 4 multicenter, single-arm, open-label trials<br>• 1 multicenter, two-arm, randomized trial |
| Phase 3 | None |
| Final Safety Database | 511 patients from 6 clinical trials |
| Were pediatric studies done or was a waiver requested? | Safety and efficacy not determined in pediatric populations. |
| Nonclinical Studies | Genotoxicity—4 *in vitro* and 1 *in vivo* tests<br>Single Dose Tox—in rats and monkeys<br>Repeat Dose Tox—in rat (1 and 6 month) and monkey (1 and 9 month)<br>Reproductive and Developmental Tox—Segment II embryo-fetal development in rats and rabbits<br>Special Tox—Immunosuppressive Potential |
| Any CMC issues? | No |
| How many times was the NDA submitted before the drug/biologic was approved? | Once (Subpart H Approval) |
| If rejected after the first submission, what were the reasons for the non-approval? | N/A |
| How long was it between the 1st NDA submission and final approval of the drug? | First Filing Date:  Dec 28, 2005<br>Approval Date:  June 28, 2006<br>Approval Time:  6 months |
| What was the tone of the communication with the agency? | Informal to formal, to the point, business-like |
| What were the proposed and final trade names? | Proposed trade names: Sprycel™<br>Final trade name: Sprycel™ |

by looking at past and present clinical trials for the compound on the therapeutic area posted on Clinicaltrials.gov or other clinical trial posting portals

• company press releases, financial statements and press—public, and sometimes non-public companies announce a lot of information about their drug development programs, but it can take time to gather this material (alternatively, there are databases that offer this "snapshot" development data; see Chapter 12 Strategy for more details)

• drug is approved in one country but not others–this drug approval package can be mined for data once it is issued

## For-Fee Tools

If the RI professional does not have the time to conduct the analysis, there are tools available to provide the individual analysis so the data can be combined as needed for the analysis, including:

- IDRAC'S Cortellis
- Tarius
- Citeline's Pipeline (formerly Pharmaprojects)
- Sagient Research BioMed Tracker
- PharmaPendium

## Fee Tools: PharmaPendium

PharmaPendium can assist in gathering regulatory information as it applies to strategy and past precedents. This tool is from MDL Information Systems Inc. (Elsevier MDL). PharmaPendium has compiled all FDA and EMA approval packages and, through the use of optical character recognition, has made these PDF documents searchable, which makes finding information across all approval packages as easy as defining the search strategy and clicking a button.

How is PharmaPendium different from what is available on the FDA or EMA website? The FDA and EMA websites can return widely scattered results when searching for key terms, and key term searches within approval packages currently are not available, especially for the older, often illegible reviews. The task of reviewing search results from the FDA and EMA websites requires wading through pages and pages of irrelevant information, with the possibility of finding what is needed. With PharmaPendium, reviews are fully searchable and results are highlighted in the text, which means exact information can be found much more quickly.

### What Can This Tool Provide?

- quick review of an FDA or EMA package based on key terms
- the pharmacokinetic profile meta-analysis based on a drug (this is a separate PharmPendium feature)
- review packages based on a generic drug name (helps find references to the drug in other packages) to help find information

across FDA and EMA if they share the same USAN and INN names
- information for developing a strategy (clinical, medical, chemistry or pharmacology) on what to do and what not to do in a development program, based on past precedents for the drug class
- review meeting minutes and what has been negotiated previously with the agency
- background on reviewers, their decisions and what they like to see or not see in an NDA
- Establishment Inspection Reports and clinical inspections and their ramifications for an NDA review, including physicians and site names
- information on a drug product, including all NDAs or ANDAs ever approved, so a complete picture is available for review

**Real Life Example**
The author was asked to create a list of drugs in a specific class that received Priority Review. "Drug class name and priority review" was entered into the database, and the search results showed the filings of those drugs that received Priority Review in the class. It then was possible to look in those specific reviews and search for the basis of the Priority Review because the text had been converted to optical character recognition. This could have been accomplished the long way, determining all the drugs in the class by looking at drugs.com and pulling up those individual filings at Drugs@FDA to find their filing review designation. Then it would have been necessary to pull up the administrative and medical sections looking for the basis of the Priority Review. Time saved? Anywhere from five to 10 hours.

## Free Tools

If a company does not have the resources for the for-fee tools, the RI professional can go to the health agency websites and

**Table 6-3. Example of Detailed Precedence Summary**

| Sponsor | Allergan Inc. | |
|---|---|---|
| NDA # | 21-023 | |
| Trade Name | RESTASIS | |
| Drug Name | Cyclosporine. Cyclosporine or CSA is an immunosuppressive agent when administered systemically and is thought to act in this indication as a partial immunomodulator. | |
| Indication | RESTASIS is indicated to increase tear production in patients whose tear production is presumed to be suppressed due to ocular inflammation associated with keratoconjunctivitis sicca (KCS).<br><br>Increased tear production was not seen in patients currently taking topical anti-inflammatory drugs or using punctual plugs. | |
| Dosage Form | Cyclosporine ophthalmic emulsion, 0.05% | |
| Classification | 505(b)(1) | |
| Mechanism of Action | CSA inhibits both humoral and cell-mediated immunity. It is effective in chronic immune-mediated inflammatory conditions and inhibition of graft rejection. The effect of CSA has been demonstrated in several inflammatory conditions, including autoimmune uveitis, psoriasis, idiopathic nephrotic syndrome and rheumatoid arthritis.<br><br>CSA inhibits the function of T lymphocytes without affecting the function of phagocytes or hemopoietic stem cells. The mechanism of CSA involves inhibition of cytokine release from the helper T cells. CSA binds with cytosolic protein known as cyclophilin. The CSA-cyclophilin complex inhibits calcium calmodulin-dependent protein calcineurine. Inhibition of calcineurine phosphatase activity by CSA-cyclophilin complex contributes to the inhibition of the function transcription factors, e.g., NFAT and NfxB. The inhibition of the nucleotide regulatory factors results in the down regulation of the cytokine gene expression. CSA also has antagonistic effect on prolactin. It is suggested that inhibition of prolactin contributes to the anti-inflammatory effect of CSA. | |
| Approved | December 23, 2002 | |
| Regulatory History | | |
| | October 19, 2000 | Letter from FDA stated that the submitted studies were not replicative and were insufficient to establish efficacy (the rest of the sentence is redacted).<br><br>(Allergan subsequently conducted two additional Phase 3 studies to demonstrate that studies 192371-002 and -003 are replicative and that 0.05% cyclosporine ophthalmic emulsion is effective; this response presents study data from a subpopulation of patients whose dry eye disease was inadequately controlled with tear substitutes.) |
| | March 25, 2000 | Letter from FDA says there is lack of substantial evidence of adequate and well-controlled investigations—insufficient to establish efficacy. |
| | August 3, 1999 | Letter from FDA states:<br>"Submitted studies are not replicative and insufficient…..(redacted)<br>Methods, facilities and controls used for the manufacture, processing, packing or holding of the drug substance or the drug product are inadequate to preserve identity, strength, quality, purity, stability and bioavailability." |
| | February 24, 1999 | Original NDA submitted |
| | | Cyclosporine 0.2% is approved as an ophthalmic ointment for the treatment of chronic KCS in dogs |

| | |
|---|---|
| **Background of Dry Eye and Cyclosporine Use in Indication** | KCS, commonly referred to as dry eye, is a disease affecting the ocular surface, the tear film and related ocular tissues and organs. The ocular surface is supported and maintained by the tear film, which is composed of 3 distinct components (lipid, aqueous and mucin) that make up 2 fluid layers. Meibomian glands along the upper and lower lid margins produce the outer lipid layer of the tear film. The inner layer, an aqueous and mucin mixture, is composed of aqueous fluid produced by the main and accessory lacrimal glands and mucins produced by goblet cells on the conjunctival epithelium as well as corneal epithelial cells.<br><br>The dry eye category characterized by aqueous deficiency can be further divided into patients with Sjogren's syndrome (a systemic autoimmune disease) and those with KCS in the absence of any related systemic disease (non-Sjogren's KCS).<br><br>The sponsor's present application considers an ophthalmic formulation of cyclosporine for the treatment of moderate to severe keratoconjunctivitis sicca. The active component of the formulation, cyclosporine, is expected to be beneficial to patients through its ability to modulate the immune reactivity and inflammatory processes. |
| **Phase 2** | One large Phase 2 |
| **Phase 3** | 4 multicenter trials; originally 2 were submitted in the original NDA, and subsequently 2 additional trials were needed to replicate results of the first 2 trials<br><br>This effect was seen in appx. 15% of RESTASIS patients versus 5% of vehicle treated patients. |
| **Adverse Events** | The most common AE reported was ocular burning (17%). |
| **Phase 3: Endpoints** | Patients demonstrated statistically significant increases in Schirmer wetting scores of 10 mm vs. vehicle at 6 months in patients whose tear production was suppressed due to ocular inflammation. |
| **Overall Clinical Conclusions** | 1) A clinically relevant, dry eye population (ITT—ocular anti-inflammatory Rx and punctal plugs) demonstrated statistically significant differences in responder rates for the number of patients who achieved an increase in Schirmer wetting scores ≥ 10mm at the 6-month time point in 192371-002 and -003.<br><br>Although -501 and -503 analyses did not achieve statistical significance, the responder analyses are supportive of the findings in -002 and -003.<br><br>2) Regarding validation of this clinical sign:<br><br>Both the OSDI symptom subscale and the OSDI overall score are statistically significantly lower in subjects with Schirmer wetting scores of ≥ 11mm in the validation studies. There also are statistically significantly lower corneal staining scores in subjects with Schirmer wetting scores of ≥ 11 mm in the validation studies.<br><br>3) Allergan has successfully demonstrated that the clinical sign (increase in Schirmer wetting scores ≥ 10mm at the 6-month time point) is clinically relevant. Lower Schirmer scores seem to have more disability due to dry eye and more ocular surface staining. |
| **Significant Protocol Violations** | • prohibited diseases (severe acne rosacea, severe migraine, Grave's disease)<br><br>• prohibited surgeries during study<br><br>• use of prohibited medications for surgeries<br><br>• use of prohibited ocular ointments, pilocarpine, ocular NSAJD, beta-blocker or ocular steroids |
| **Final Safety Database** | ≈1600 with moderate to severe keratoconjunctivitis sicca |
| **Were pediatric studies done or was a waiver requested?** | No, waiver applied for and approved. |

| Nonclinical Studies | Most studies were literature references or based on NDA 50-733, 50-574, 50-573 (Novartis NDAs for cyclosporine) |
|---|---|
| | 1. A 6-month ocular and systemic toxicity study with a 2-month recovery period in New Zealand white rabbits. Report 1793-2936-6. |
| | 2. A 52-week ocular and systemic study of cyclosporine in dogs with an 8-week recovery period. Report 985-126. |
| | 3. A 6-month interim toxicokinetic report: Pharmacokinetic analysis of Cyclosporine A in dog blood for study 985-126, 52-week ocular and systemic study of cyclosporine in dogs with an 8-week recovery period. Report PK-96-001. |
| | 4. The blood to plasma concentration ratio of JH-Cyclosporine-A in mouse, rat, rabbit, dog and human in vitro. Report PK-94-108. |
| | 5. Ocular pharmacokinetics of cyclosporine after a single eye drop instillation of a 0.2% 3H-cyclosporine ophthalmic emulsion into albino rabbit eyes. Study PK-95-010. |
| | 6. Investigation of ocular metabolism of cyclosporine after a single drop instillation of a 0.2% 3H cyclosporine ophthalmic emulsion into albino rabbit eyes. Study PK-95-011. |
| | 7. Pharmacokinetic kinetic analysis of Cyclosporine A in rabbit blood for study #1793-2936-6. AGN 192371-Cyclosporine ophthalmic emulsion: A 6-month ocular and systemic toxicity study with a 2-month recovery period in New Zealand white rabbits. Study PK-95-066. |
| | 8. The effect of oil globule size on ocular absorption of $^3$H-Cyclosporine after topical instillation of three 0.2% 3H-cyclosporine oil-in-water emulsions into rabbit eyes. Report PK-95-074. |
| | 9. Dose proportionality of ocular tissue $^3$H-Cyclosporine concentrations after a single dose administration of 0.05%, 0.2% and 0.4% H-Cyclosporine emulsions into rabbit eyes. Report PK-96-011. |
| | 10. Ocular absorption and disposition in beagle dogs following multiple ocular doses of 0.2% $^3$H Cyclosporine emulsion. Report PK-96-016. |
| | 11. Ocular absorption and disposition in beagle dogs following single ocular doses of 0.2% $^3$H Cyclosporine emulsion. Report PK-96-017. |
| | 12. Pharmacokinetic analysis of cyclosporine in dog blood for 52-week ocular systemic study of cyclosporine in dogs with an 8-week recovery period. Report PK-96-023. |
| | 13. Ocular cyclosporine distribution during 9 ~ days of dosing of 0.05% and 0.1% $^3$H-Cyclosporine A emulsions to albino rabbits. Report PK-98-074. |
| | 14. Cyclosporine A PA-1998-0l0, special study. |

see whether the marketing application review is posted. Marketing application reviews are posted by a limited number of agencies, including the US FDA, EU EMA (centrally authorized products only), United Kingdom's Medicines and Healthcare products Regulatory Agency (MHRA), Irish Medicines Board (IMB), Australian TGA, Health Canada and Japan's PMDA. FDA provides the most extensive product review information due to transparency initiatives, but quality information typically is limited, while EMA provides a nice background and more product quality data. Summaries provided by TGA, Health Canada, MHRA, IMB and PMDA are rather limited but do indicate the product was approved in the country.

Websites of interest include:
- US FDA's Drugs@FDA, www.accessdata.fda.gov/scripts/cder/drugsatfda/
- EMA EPARs, www.ema.europa.eu/ema/index.jsp?curl=/pages/medicines/landing/epar_search.jsp&mid=WC0b01ac058001d124
- JAPAN, RAD-AR or Risk-Benefit Assessment of Drug Analysis www.rad-ar.or.jp/siori/english/index.html
- Health Canada Summary Basis of Decision (SBD), www.hc-sc.gc.ca/dhp-mps/prodpharma/sbd-smd/drug-med/index-eng.php
- TGA's AusPARs, www.tga.gov.au/industry/pm-auspar.htm#.UsCwLLQ-ZZI

## When are reviews available on agency websites?

### FDA (21 CFR 20.117)

- Action packages must be posted to the FDA website within 30 days of approval for new chemical entities (NCEs) and not later than 30 days after the third *Freedom of Information Act (FOIA)* request for an SBA for any other drug.
- Within 48 hours of approval (except in cases of redaction), a "summary review that documents conclusions from all reviewing disciplines about the drug, noting any critical issues and disagreements with the applicant....." must be posted.
- Although not updated during the product lifecycle, additional approval letters, labels and sometimes supplements are added to the database.
- For products that have been submitted but not approved, no information is made available.

### EMA (REGULATION (EC) No. 726/2004)

- Pending decisions are posted.
- Any positive opinion given by the Committee for Medicinal Products for Human Use (CHMP) is published in the first instance as a summary of opinion soon after the opinion is given. More detailed information is published later as an EPAR, following the granting of a Marketing Authorisation by the European Commission.
- EPAR summaries are limited to centrally authorized products.
- EPARs are updated as information about the product changes.
- For a Marketing Authorisation that has been submitted and withdrawn or for which a negative opinion was issued or the application refused, a summary is posted.

## How to Put Together Past Precedent Information

First, the information needed and why must be defined; it helps to lay it out in a table format. Once the information is defined, sources need to identified and information collected.

The final step is opening and reading the posted reviews and filling in the predefined sections in the table.

See **Table 6-1** for an example of a worksheet that can be used to start collecting data or as a high-level summary. **Table 6-2** is a high-level summary and **Table 6-3** is a very detailed precedent summary (although this has been shorted for publication and a summary should be more extensive that the example shown).

## What to Summarize in a Drug Review

When a drug is approved or when conducting a past precedent review, what typically is sought and summarized?

- clinical endpoints and label claims
  - o How many studies were conducted to support approval?
  - o What indications were studied?
  - o What were the study designs and investigational phases?
  - o What were the endpoints and were they met?
  - o What were the target populations (age/country/gender)?
  - o What comparators were used?
  - o Who were the clinical investigators?
  - o Were there GXP compliance issues?
  - o Were there safety issues (e.g., clinical hold)?
  - o Did the agency agree with their endpoints or make alternative suggestions and why?
- types of nonclinical trials conducted
  - o How many and what types of studies were conducted to support the indication?

- o Were any significant safety signals seen? If so, how were they mitigated?
- o Did the agency request any special kinds of studies?
- o Were any waivers requested or received?
- o Were there any Special Protocol Assessments for carcinogenicity?
- labeling and trade names
  - o What were the clinical studies' indications and the final label claim? Were they the same or different and why?
  - o Were there any labeling negotiations? If so, what are the differences between what the company wanted and the final label?
  - o Is there class labeling?
  - o Were there any naming issues?
- DEA scheduling issues
- REMS—Was there a requirement for a? If so, what were the product-specific or class requirements?
- quality challenges—stability data submitted and commitments, shelf life obtained
- regulatory history and barriers—development issues and how they were resolved
- waivers obtained, if any
- tone and type of agency communication
- any nonstandard requests by the agency
- regulatory pathway followed
- number of review cycles
- if applicable, why a complete response letter or refuse to file letter was initially issued
- agency reviewers, have they reviewed similar products and any specific questions or issues with this program[1]
- any regulation change or guidance document issuance resulting from the filing or the drug development plan

However, what ultimately is reviewed, found and summarized will depend on the therapeutic area and goal of the research.

References
1. DIA RIM Presentation, "Precedent and its Significance in Developing Regulatory Strategy" by Linda Bowen, February 3, 2013.

# CHAPTER 7

# Freedom of Information (FOI) and Right to Information (RTI) Request Overview

## What is FOI?

The US *Freedom of Information Act (FOI or FOIA)* and Right to Information (RTI) laws outside the US give citizens the right to access information from governments. Many countries have an act similar to *FOIA*, but this chapter focuses on the US and FDA. However, links to global FOI websites can be found in **Table 7-1**.

In the US, *FOIA* (www.foia.gov and www.fda.gov/RegulatoryInformation/FOI/default.htm) was enacted in 1966, and took effect on 5 July 1967. There were major amendments in 1996—the *Electronic Freedom of Information Act Amendments* mandated publicly accessible "electronic reading rooms" and other information routinely available to the public, with electronic search and indexing features. Further amendments were added in 2007 by Public Law 110-175, *The Openness Promotes Effectiveness in our National Government Act* of 2007. During the Obama administration, to increase transparency, the *Open Government Initiative* (21 January 2009) was passed. This created a much more open and transparent FDA by mandating that the agency provide the public with useful, user-friendly

information about agency activities and decision making. FOI is regulated by 21 CFR 20.

*FOIA* generally provides that any person has the right, enforceable in court, to access federal agency records, except to the extent that the records (or portions of those records) are protected from public disclosure by one of the exemptions (specifically nine exemptions) or by one of three special law enforcement record exclusions contained within *FOIA*, or under an agency's implementing regulations.

FDA's FOI program is decentralized, and personnel process requests across all agency components. These employees respond to requests from the public and must locate and review records for deletion of nonpublic information pursuant to the regulations and the *FOIA* exemptions. The Division of Freedom of Information (DFOI) functions as the administrative headquarters for the agency's FOI program. Among other functions, DFOI also serves as the point of contact for the requester public and ensures FDA offices release information consistent with the relevant statutes, regulations and policies.

Why is FOI used in RI activities? Because the records RI professionals

**Table 7-1. Listing of Global FOI sites**

| An overview of each country's laws | http://en.wikipedia.org/wiki/Freedom_of_information_laws_by_country |
|---|---|
| In-depth description of the global laws | http://www.freedominfo.org/documents/global_survey2006.pdf |
| Table of comparison of laws | http://www.justice.tas.gov.au/__data/assets/pdf_file/0004/118930/Table_of_Global_Comparison_of_FoI_Laws.pdf |
| Canadian FOI Resource Site | http://www3.telus.net/index100/foi |

are looking for, like an Establishment Inspection Report (EIR) or a Summary Basis of Approval (SBA) for a 505(b)(2) product, are not posted. Some records are not included on the FDA website until they are requested for the third time.

## What is publically available?

Before asking FDA for information, the RI professional needs to know what is available without an FOI request (although some material might not be timely):
- compliance information
  - EIRs, Form 483s, Untitled Letters, Warning Letters, Notices of Opportunity for Hearing (NOOHs) and Notices of Initiation of Disqualification Proceedings and Opportunity to Explain (NIDPOEs)
- approval information
  - Advisory Committee briefing information and meetings
  - approval packages, SBAs (Drugs@FDA)
  - device clearances and approvals (510(k)s and PMAs)
- patent and exclusivity information for drugs (*Orange Book*)
- Risk Evaluation and Mitigation Strategies (REMS)
- company postmarketing requirements and commitments
- recalls (The Enforcement Report), market withdrawals and safety alerts
- inactive ingredient database
- dissolution methods database
- database of registered establishments

- National Institute of Health's ClinicalTrials.gov
- comments to proposed rules and draft guidance documents, Citizen's Petitions, Suitability Petitions (Federal Dockets Management System)
- pediatric trial information

For a complete listing of all electronic reading rooms and publically available data, please see: http://www.fda.gov/regulatoryinformation/foi/electronicreadingroom/default.htm.

FDA posts the most frequently requested documents to these reading rooms. Typically, after a document is requested three times (if not mandated to be posted), FDA posts it. If the RI professional is aware or believes a document exists and wants a copy of it, if not already posted on the FDA website, it is necessary to send an FOI request for the document(s).

## What typically is not available?

FDA usually does not disclose any information about the existence, status or content of an application submitted to the agency until the product has been approved, licensed or cleared. Statutes and FDA regulations generally prohibit the release of information from or about an unapproved application. This includes:[1,2]
- Investigational New Drugs (INDs) or Investigational Device Exemptions (IDEs)
- INDs or IDEs on clinical hold
- complete marketing applications and supplements (New Drug Applications (NDAs), Abbreviated New Drug

Applications (ANDAs) and Biologics License Applications (BLAs)) or those still under review
- Refusal to File information
- issuance of a complete response letter
- unapproved drug or uncleared 510(k) that has been withdrawn

## Typical RI FOI Topics

What are the typical items not on FDA's website that an RI professional can request under *FOIA*? Everything and anything including:
- summaries and reviews of approved marketing submissions
- EIRs and Warning Letters
- clinical site inspection reports
- NIDPOE letters
- efficacy supplement medical review
- manufacturing supplement review
- postmarketing commitment study medical review

Requests may be submitted for a single record from one component or potentially can involve thousands of pages of records from multiple offices depending on the request.

## What cannot be requested?

RI professionals can request anything they want to know about, but that does not mean FDA will release the information.[3]

## Information Exemptions

Once FDA decides a document should be denied, it is unlikely it would overturn that position on appeal. An FOI denial can be appealed in writing within 60 days of receiving the initial denial letter. Nine exemptions exist that form the basis for denial of FOI requests, meaning information will not be released. The six exemptions most frequently used as the basis for FDA withholding information are in bold:

1. classified national defense and foreign relations information
2. **internal agency rules and practice**
3. **information prohibited from disclosure by another law**
4. **trade secrets and other confidential business information**
5. **inter-agency or intra-agency communications protected by legal privileges**
6. **information involving matters of personal privacy**
7. **certain information compiled for law enforcement purposes**
8. information relating to the supervision of financial institutions
9. geological information on wells

Even if information is exempt from disclosure under *FOIA*, the agency still may disclose it as a matter of administrative discretion if it chooses to do so, and disclosure of that information is not prohibited by any law. Information deemed proprietary can be redacted from the document (this means a document may have most of the page blacked out but the FOI request has been fulfilled).

## What needs to be included in an FOI request?

With regard to an FOI request, the more detail provided, the more quickly the request will be fulfilled. All FOI requests must be in writing, but can now be submitted electronically at www.accessdata. fda.gov/scripts/foi/FOIRequest/request-info.cfm; if FOI requests are submitted frequently, FDA requests the company to set up an account. No oral requests will be honored. The request should include the following:
- Requester's name, address and telephone number
- A description of the records being sought enables them to be identified and located—the records should be identified as specifically as possible. A request for specific records that are releasable to the public can be processed much

**Figure 7-1. FOI Request Letter Example**

---

Date

Food and Drug Administration
Office of Management Programs
Division of Freedom of Information (HFI-35)
5600 Fishers Lane
Rockville, MD 20857
RE: **Request for Existing Records under the Freedom of Information Act**

Dear Sir or Madam,

Pursuant to 21 CFR § 20.23, we hereby request the documents identified below that are existing records of the agency.

All written notices from the agency to clinical investigators pursuant to 21 CFR § 312.70 (often referred to as "Notice of Initiation of Disqualification Proceedings and Opportunity to Explain (NIDPOE) Letters") issued on or after May 18, 2006 and on or before December 31, 2007 to the extent that they have not already been made publicly available in FDA's Electronic Reading Room website http://www.fda.gov/foi/nidpoe/default.html.

It is noted that the last letter posted on the Electronic Reading Room website was issued on 18 May 2006.

I make this request in my capacity as an employee of (insert company name) for use in connection with the company's business. I understand that there may be fees charged for some or all of the costs of processing this request. I respectfully request that the agency contact me using the contact information provided below if the maximum dollar amount of any fees exceeds $250.00.

I can be reached at (insert phone number and email).

Signed,


Regulatory Representative Name

---

*Please note the example given above is for the US FOI system; requirements and results vary by country but can be similar.*

more quickly than a request for "all information" on a particular subject, since such an ambiguous request will incur a charge for "research time." Language used in the request should cite the applicable law and carefully explain the reasons for seeking the information.

o If the description is not sufficient to locate the records requested, FDA will so notify the requester and indicate the additional information needed to identify those records.

• Separate requests should be submitted for each firm or product involved (i.e., requests should not be combined).
• A statement concerning willingness to pay fees, including any limitations—if the fees exceed the maximum amount stated, FDA will contact the requester before fulfilling the request. Requesters generally are billed for fees after their requests have been processed; however, if total fees are expected to exceed $250, FDA may

require payment in advance of processing.

See **Figures 7-1** and **7-2** for request letter examples.

## Submitting Requests Online

Following is the process when submitting an online request
- Enter a valid email address.
- Enter a complete description of the request in the subject field.
- An electronic copy of the request letter may be attached to the request form.
- Multiple requests may be entered without re-entering the requester information.
- After the request is submitted, the requester will receive a confirmation number and be able to print a copy of the request.
- After acceptance by FDA's FOI staff, an electronic acknowledgement letter with the FOI control number will be sent to the email address provided in the request.

## Where to Send FOI Requests

Written FOI requests should be sent to:
Food and Drug Administration
Division of Freedom of Information
Office of the Executive Secretariat, OC
12420 Parklawn Drive
ELEM-1029
Rockville, MD 20857

Alternatively, the request can be faxed to +1 301 827 9267 or +1 301 796 3900.

Questions on *FOIA* can be directed to the Freedom of Information Offices at +1 301 796 3900.

If a requester wants help, it is possible to have the letter generated by visiting www.ifoia.org/#!/.

## What Happens After an FOI Request is Submitted

Once the FOI office receives the request, it is registered in the FOI log book (which is available for public disclosure and viewing), and an acknowledgement letter about the request will be sent to the requester, providing a tracking number, typically within 20 days. This acknowledgement letter states the agency's determination as to whether, or the extent to which, the agency will comply with the request and, if any records are denied, the reasons for the denial.

The "log book" entry will include the date received, the requester's name, the nature of the record requested, the action taken on the request, the date of determination and the date(s) any records are subsequently furnished. Copies of the "log book" can be requested to see who requested what records; this allows an RI professional to track what competitors are requesting.

If the request is for a document in FOI staff control, such as copies of previously released FOI documents already having assigned FOI control numbers, the request usually is fulfilled immediately. If they cannot fulfill the request, FOI staff then send the request to the appropriate division, and the division makes the decision on whether the records are releasable. In addition, center, division or office staff are responsible for locating the document and determining whether it can be fully disclosed or needs to be redacted. If the division cannot fulfill the request, it sends the request to a regional or district office where the document is maintained. Eventually, the document is sent to the requester. The delivery of the information can be a few weeks to years, depending on its availability and whether it has been requested previously.

## Situations in Which Confidentiality is Uncertain

In situations where the confidentiality of data or information is uncertain and there is a request for public disclosure, FDA

**Figure 7-2. Fax Request Example**

---

**Facsimile Message**

**To:** FDA, FOI Staff    at    301-443-1726/301-443-1719

**From:** Regulatory    at    Phone

**Date:** Enter date

**Subject:** **FOI Request for an Establishment Inspection Report (EIR)**

**Pages (Including Cover):** 1

Dear FOI Staff:

I would like to request a copy of the following document:

| Type of Document: | Establishment Inspection Report (EIR) |
| --- | --- |
| Name of Company: | Sicor S.r.l. |
| Location: | Rho (Milan), Italy |
| Date of Inspection: | March 2007 (inspection was from the 12th to 14th) |
| Name of FDA Inspector: | Uduak Inokon |
| What was Inspected: | Active Pharmaceutical Ingredient Manufacturing Facility |

We would like the whole report, not just the narrative portion.

I make this request in my capacity as an employee of (insert company name) for use in connection with the company's business. I understand that there may be fees charged for some or all of the costs of processing this request. I respectfully request that the agency contact me using the contact information provided below if the maximum dollar amount of any fees exceeds $250.00.

If you have any questions, you can reach me at (insert phone number and email). Thank you.

Sincerely,

Regulatory Representative

---

*Please note the example given above is for the US FOI system; requirements and results vary by country but can be similar.*

will consult the person who submitted or divulged the data or information or would be affected by disclosure before determining whether such data or information is available for public disclosure.

## Timeline for Information to be Received

Requesters who need the information right away think because they have requested it, the information should be sent immediately. Receiving a confirmation letter in 20 days does not mean the information will be delivered in 20 days. The letter is an acknowledgement that a request has been made.

- According to FDA's Fiscal 2012 FOI "progress report:"
  - o Median processing time for simple requests was 32 days; average time was 78.7 days.

o Median processing time for complex requests was 136 days; average time was 192.1.

o Status of pending requests—2,863 www.access-data.fda.gov/FDATrack/track?program=foia&id=FOIA-Number-of-FOIA-requests-pending and www.hhs.gov/foia/reports/13anlrpt.html

## FOI Denial Statistics

In 2013, the agency fully denied only 194 requests out of a total of 9,990, which means most requests will be fulfilled eventually.

## FOI Appeals

An FOI requester may appeal the denial of records in response to a request.

The appeal must be in writing and be sent to the review official at the address provided within the time limit in the denial letter.

The appeal letter should state the reasons the *FOI* exemption(s) cited does not apply to the records requested or give reasons why the document(s) should be released regardless of whether the exemption(s) apply.

If the review official grants the appeal, FDA will provide access to the records or explain the reason for delay. If the decision denies the appeal, the official will state the reasons for the decision in writing and inform the requester of the *FOI* provision for judicial review.

## FOI Vendors—What to Do When the Information is Needed Quickly

To get a document posted on FDA's website if its posting is not mandated, it needs to be requested three times. If help is needed with the request or to get the document released sooner, an FOI vendor can be solicited to make another request. Additionally, FOI vendors have request tricks based on years of experience requesting documents. These vendors, like foiservices.com, also might already have the documents in their databases, so when the requester needs a document quickly, they can help for a fee.

## Managing Multiple FOI Requests

If a company makes frequent requests to the FOI Document Room, the FOI office could ask that it limits its requests to certain days of the week to help manage the large influx of requests.

The requester will need to develop a database to help manage and track large numbers of FOI requests so they and ultimately the associated invoices will not be duplicated, and FOI requests, once received, can be routed to the proper personnel.

## Submission of Records Marked as Confidential

Some sponsors think marking submission documents "confidential" will, in fact, keep the information confidential and not allow its release. In fact, marking submissions as confidential, or any similar term, creates no obligation by FDA to regard such records as confidential, to return them to the person who has submitted them, to withhold them from disclosure to the public or to advise the person submitting them when a request for public disclosure is received or they are in fact disclosed. If the public requests a document, FDA has the discretion to decide whether to release it even if it is marked "confidential."

Additionally, records submitted to FDA may not be withdrawn. All FDA records are retained by the agency until disposed of pursuant to routine record disposal procedures.

References
1. The FDA Transparency Initiative and Access to Information, Linda Bowen, DIA RIM 2012.
2. The FDA Transparency Initiative and Access to Information & Disclosure: FOIA Requests, Marlene Bobka, DIA RIM 2013.
3. Ibid.

CHAPTER 8

# Advisory Committee Meetings and Member Profiles

## What are Advisory Committee Meetings?

Per 21 CFR 10.3, a Public Advisory Committee or Advisory Committee (AdCom) means any committee, board, commission, council, conference, panel, task force or other similar group, or any subcommittee or other subgroup of an Advisory Committee, that is not composed wholly of full-time employees of the federal government and is established or utilized by FDA to obtain advice or recommendations. In other words, AdCom meetings are a public discussion involving FDA, the sponsor, outside experts and the public.

## Why are AdCom Meetings needed?

FDA's Advisory Committees provide independent expert advice to the agency on a range of complex scientific, technical and policy issues related to human and veterinary drugs, biological products, medical devices and food. An AdCom Meeting also provides a forum for a public airing of important matters concerning agency policies and FDA-regulated medical products. AdCom Meetings are needed for:

- New Molecular Entities (NMEs)
- difficult benefit-risk ratio questions
- interpretation of efficacy results
- disagreement between sponsor and FDA
- prescription to over-the-counter switch
- broad public health implications and/or discussions
- guidance development

From a regulatory perspective, AdCom Meetings:

- establish, in a public forum, the opinion of the practicing physician
- provide transparency of the regulatory process
- offer the ability to be represented and influence opinion
- speed up the review process over issues that might have been roadblocks

From FDA's perspective, these meetings:

- provide scientific knowledge and real-world advice

- provide support on tough decisions

From the public's perspective, these meetings:
- get needed medicines approved for unmet medical needs
- allow their voices to be heard and influence the regulatory process

## What can be learned from an Advisory Committee Meeting?

Although the committees provide advice to the agency, final decisions are made by FDA.

The basis for FDA's decision to approve or not approve a product application should be understood by the public, especially where FDA does not follow that advice (in post-meeting minutes and transcripts), to help the public better understand the agency's action. Disclosing this information leads to a better understanding of the basis for FDA's decisions, increases agency accountability and credibility in its decision making and furthers the federal initiative for a more transparent and accountable government.

From an industry perspective, it is possible to learn specific product's details prior to approval, which typically are not available due to confidentiality regulations. From an AdCom Meeting, a company can learn about a competitor's product, the data the sponsor has to support its marketing application, the problems with its marketing application and FDA's concerns prior to the NDA being approved.

## How do you find out about an AdCom Meeting?

All public AdCom Meetings are announced in the *Federal Register*—another reason to read this daily journal from the US government (FDA-specific portions of the *Federal Register* can be found at www.federalregister.gov/agencies/food-and-drug-administration; it also is possible to subscribe to the daily journal on this site).

Another way to find out about upcoming meetings is to visit FDA's Advisory Committee Calendar page at www.fda.gov/AdvisoryCommittees/Calendar/default.htm. It is possible to sign up on this page for e-mail notifications of upcoming meetings; this results in notifications of all meetings, not just ones of particular interest. To be notified of upcoming meetings, register with FDA for notification (www.fda.gov/AboutFDA/ContactFDA/StayInformed/GetEmailUpdates/default.htm) or RSS feeds www.fda.gov/AboutFDA/ContactFDA/StayInformed/RSSFeeds/default.htm) to receive all meeting announcements.

If the meeting is of particular importance, it also might be mentioned in a trade journal with background on why the meeting is important and what precedents will be established at the meeting.

## What information can be found prior to the meeting?

Prior to the meeting, the following can be found online:
- AdCom Meeting announcements—tentative and scheduled
- meeting materials (briefing material from both FDA and the sponsor)
- slides
- agenda
- meeting roster
- waivers for conflicts of interest (if applicable)
- committee charter
- membership roster

After the meeting has concluded, a meeting summary and transcript are posted.

To find this material, go to the committee's website and find the meeting date. The meeting information and date will allow the RI professional to develop a regulatory history based on clinical trial results and challenges for the product, coupled with any press releases (if available). A day or two prior to the meeting, the company's data package will be posted along with FDA's interpretation and stance on the data (FDA's briefing package). Reading this background helps the RI professional develop and anticipate FDA's position and the company's challenges going into the meeting. This data and the meeting outcome will help the RI analyst apply the information to his or her current development programs or anticipate questions and issues in an upcoming AdCom meeting for his or her company.

Following are examples of typical documents posted pre- and post-meeting, in this instance for the 7 December 2012 meeting of the Anesthetic and Analgesic Drug Products Advisory Committee:

- meeting announcement (www.fda.gov/AdvisoryCommittees/Calendar/ucm327624.htm)
- draft agenda (www.fda.gov/downloads/AdvisoryCommittees/CommitteesMeetingMaterials/Drugs/AnestheticAndAnalgesicDrugProductsAdvisoryCommittee/UCM330676.pdf)
- draft questions (www.fda.gov/downloads/AdvisoryCommittees/CommitteesMeetingMaterials/Drugs/AnestheticAndAnalgesicDrugProductsAdvisoryCommittee/UCM330677.pdf)
- draft meeting roster (www.fda.gov/downloads/AdvisoryCommittees/CommitteesMeetingMaterials/Drugs/AnestheticAndAnalgesicDrugProductsAdvisoryCommittee/UCM330678.pdf)
- committee roster (www.fda.gov/downloads/AdvisoryCommittees/CommitteesMeetingMaterials/Drugs/AnestheticAndAnalgesicDrugProductsAdvisoryCommittce/UCM330679.pdf)
- briefing information (www.fda.gov/AdvisoryCommittees/CommitteesMeetingMaterials/Drugs/AnestheticAndAnalgesicDrugProductsAdvisoryCommittee/ucm330681.htm)
- webcast information (www.fda.gov/downloads/AdvisoryCommittees/CommitteesMeetingMaterials/Drugs/AnestheticAndAnalgesicDrugProductsAdvisoryCommittee/UCM330680.pdf)
- final agenda (www.fda.gov/downloads/AdvisoryCommittees/CommitteesMeetingMaterials/Drugs/AnestheticAndAnalgesicDrugProductsAdvisoryCommittee/UCM333210.pdf)
- final questions (www.fda.gov/downloads/AdvisoryCommittees/CommitteesMeetingMaterials/Drugs/AnestheticAndAnalgesicDrugProductsAdvisoryCommittee/UCM333212.pdf)
- final meeting roster (www.fda.gov/downloads/AdvisoryCommittees/CommitteesMeetingMaterials/Drugs/AnestheticAndAnalgesicDrugProductsAdvisoryCommittee/UCM333215.pdf)
- slides (www.fda.gov/AdvisoryCommittees/CommitteesMeetingMaterials/Drugs/AnestheticAndAnalgesicDrugProductsAdvisoryCommittee/ucm333217.htm)
- minutes (www.fda.gov/downloads/AdvisoryCommittees/CommitteesMeetingMaterials/Drugs/AnestheticAndAnalgesicDrugProductsAdvisoryCommittee/UCM336475.pdf)
- transcript (www.fda.gov/downloads/AdvisoryCommittees/CommitteesMeetingMaterials/Drugs/AnestheticAndAnalgesicDrugProductsAdvisoryCommittee/UCM339619.pdf)

## How and where can AdCom Meeting information be found?

Upcoming meetings can be found at: www.fda.gov/AdvisoryCommittees/Calendar/default.htm

Past meetings can be found at:
- 2013—www.fda.gov/AdvisoryCommittees/Calendar/2013/default.htm
- 2012—www.fda.gov/AdvisoryCommittees/Calendar/2012/default.htm

- 2011—www.fda.gov/
  AdvisoryCommittees/
  Calendar/2011/default.htm
- 2010—www.fda.gov/
  AdvisoryCommittees/
  Calendar/2010/default.htm
- 2009—www.fda.gov/
  AdvisoryCommittees/
  Calendar/2010/default.htm
- Pre-2009—www.fda.
  gov/oc/advisory/
  accalendar/2008/2008ACcalendar.
  html

## What are AdCom Meeting summaries and who provides them?

Several vendors, including Cortellis and Tarius, provide AdCom Meeting summaries. A summary provides a complete snapshot of what happened at the meeting:
- summary and background information on the NDA
- indication sought
- regulatory history
- clinical trials conducted (high level results)
- key issues discussed regarding the NDA and product being reviewed
- related AdCom Meeting(s) and/or guidance documents
- questions asked of the committee and the voting record

FDA also provides a summary based on the transcript, but its summary tends to be issued weeks to months after the AdCom Meeting (e.g., www.fda.gov/downloads/advisorycommittees/committeesmeetingmaterials/drugs/drugsafetyandriskmanagementadvisorycommittee/ucm343936.pdf). The only way an RI professional can get a meeting summary more quickly than the one provided by a vendor is to actually attend the meeting.

## Who are AdCom members?

In general, AdComs include a chair, several members, plus consumer,

industry and, sometimes, patient group representatives. Additional experts with special knowledge may be added for individual meetings as needed. FDA has 33 AdComs, established to provide functions that support the agency's mission of protecting and promoting the public health, while meeting the requirements set forth in the *Federal Advisory Committee Act*. Committees either are mandated by statute or established at the discretion of the Department of Health and Human Services. Each committee is subject to renewal at two-year intervals unless the committee charter states otherwise. A complete listing of all AdComs can be found at www.fda.gov/AdvisoryCommittees/CommitteesMeetingMaterials/default.htm.

Each committee consists of a core of 13 voting members, including the chair. Members and the chair are selected by the FDA commissioner or her designee from among authorities knowledgeable in the fields of anesthesiology, surgery, epidemiology or statistics and related specialties. The core of voting members may include one technically qualified member, selected by the commissioner or her designee, who is identified with consumer interests and is recommended by either a consortium of consumer-oriented organizations or other interested persons. In addition to the voting members, the committee may include one non-voting member who is identified with industry interests. Each member serves for up to four years, and there are one to four meetings per year.

Vacancy and waiver statistics are available at www.fda.gov/AboutFDA/Transparency/track/ucm216403.htm.

Membership lists are found on each individual AdCom webpage, such as a committee roster (e.g., the Anesthetic and Analgesic Drug Products Advisory Committee: www.fda.gov/AdvisoryCommittees/CommitteesMeetingMaterials/Drugs/AnestheticAndAnalgesicDrugProductsAdvisoryCommittee/ucm094128.htm.).

**Table 8-1. Advisory Committee Member or Reviewer Bibliography (for a single reviewer, no questions reviewed)**

| Topic | Title/Document Information | Abstract | Application to Program |
|---|---|---|---|
| Comparator Control | Placebo-controlled trials and the *Declaration of Helsinki*<br><br>Lewis, John A.; Jonsson, Bertil; Kreutz, Gottfried; Sampaio, Cristina; van Zwieten-Boot, Barbara<br><br>Lancet<br>VOLUME 359, NUMBER 9314, 2002 Apr, PP 1337-1340 | A revised version of the *Declaration of Helsinki*, issued in October 2000, remains a vital expression of medical ethics, and deserves unanimous support. A strict interpretation of the declaration seems to rule out clinical trials that use a placebo-control group whenever licensed therapeutic methods already exist, preferring active controls. Although the efficacy of some new medicines can be satisfactorily established without the use of a placebo, for others the judicious use of placebo remains essential to establish their effectiveness. This article discusses the particular wording of Section 29 of the declaration, clinical trials of new medicinal products, advantages of placebo-controlled trials and ethically acceptable use of placebo control. | Licensed therapeutic that is equivalent to product is not available, hence the need to use a control |
| Parkinson's Disease | Health-related quality of life in multiple system atrophy<br><br>Schrag, Anette; Geser, Felix; Stampfer-Kountchev, Michaela; Seppi, Klaus; Sawires, Martin; Koellensperger, Martin; Scherfler, Christoph; Quinn, Niall; Pellecchia, Maria T; Barone, Paolo; Del Sorbo, Francesca; Albanese, Alberto; Ostergaard, Karen; Dupont, Erik; Cardozo, Adriana; Tolosa, Eduardo; Nilsson, Christer F; Widner, Hokan; Lindvall, Olle; Giladi, Nir; Gurevich, Tanya; Daniels, Christine; Deuschl, Gounther; Coelho, Miguel; Sampaio, Cristina; Abele, Michael; Klockgether, Thomas; Schimke, Nicole; Eggert, Karla M; Oertel, Wolfgang; Djaldetti, Ruth; Colosimo, Carlo; Meco, Giuseppe; Poewe, Werner; Wenning, Gregor K; European MSA-Study Group<br><br>Mov Disord<br>VOLUME 21, Number 6, 2006 June, pp 809-15 | Although multiple system atrophy (MSA) is a neurodegenerative disorder leading to progressive disability and decreased life expectancy, little is known about patients' own evaluation of their illness and factors associated with poor health-related quality of life (Hr-QoL). We, therefore, assessed Hr-QoL and its determinants in MSA. The following scales were applied to 115 patients in the European MSA-Study Group (EMSA-SG) Natural History Study: Medical Outcome Study Short Form (SF-36), EQ-5D, Beck Depression Inventory (BDI), Mini-Mental state examination (MMSE), Unified MSA Rating Scale (UMSARS), Hoehn & Yahr (H&Y) Parkinson's disease staging scale, Composite Autonomic Symptom Scale (COMPASS) and Parkinson's Disease Sleep Scale (PDSS). Forty-six percent of patients had moderate to severe depression (BDI > or = 17); Hr-QoL scores on the SF-36 and EQ-5D were significantly impaired. Pain, the only domain with similar scores in MSA and published PD patients, was reported more frequently in patients with MSA-P (predominantly parkinsonian motor subtype) than MSA-C (predominantly cerebellar motor subtype; 76% vs. 50%; P = 0.005). Hr-QoL scores correlated most strongly with UMSARS motor, COMPASS and BDI scores but not with MMSE scores, age at onset or disease duration. The COMPASS and UMSARS activities of daily living scores were moderate-to-strong predictors for the SF-36 physical summary score and the BDI and UMSARS motor scores for the SF-36 mental summary score. This report is the first study to show that Hr-QoL is significantly impaired in MSA. Although not all possible factors related to impaired Hr-QoL in MSA could be assessed, autonomic dysfunction, motor impairment and depression were most closely associated with poor Hr-QoL, and therapeutic management, therefore, should concentrate upon these aspects of the disease. | Familiarity with Quality of Life measurements |

## Member Profiles

Several vendors provide AdCom member profiles. These vendors give instant access to profiles, across many committees and keep them updated. These profiles also can be created by an RI analyst from AdCom Meeting transcripts and the curricula vitae provided for all members on the AdCom meeting site (see **Table 8-1** for a sample bibliography) and a LinkedIn and Medline literature search. Typical information included in a summary includes:

- member name
- education and employment history
- publications and areas of interest
- AdCom voting history
- typical questions or areas of focus of participation in AdCom Meetings

## Engaging Past and Present Advisory Committee Members

Past and present AdCom members are invaluable for gaining insight on the agency's current thinking and how it might react to a certain issue. Additionally, a company might need external support. If a previous AdCom member believes in the company's position, the company may ask him or her to attend a development meeting with FDA to provide the company with support on a particular topic. Because a division has experience with this previous AdCom member, it implicitly trusts the individual, which can add credibility to the company's position, especially if the topic is controversial.

CHAPTER 9

# Reviewer Profiles

## Who are the Reviewers?

Reviewers are FDA (or other regulatory health agency) employees who comprise the mirror image of a company's drug development team. The RI professional can start to learn about the review team members as soon as the attendee list for the Pre-IND Meeting is received; some of these team members also will be on the review team for the company's IND, IND amendments, NDA and NDA amendments or supplements. Therefore, it is best for the regulatory team to get to know these reviewers and understand their perspectives. It also is important for the company to know when team members change, as the reviewers on an IND can be very different than the reviewers for an NDA.

## Why Collect Reviewer Profile Information and What do you do with it?

When a company is hiring someone to join the regulatory team, it interviews individuals to learn about their background, education, skills and expertise. Unfortunately, a company does not have that advantage with the FDA review team, which will be instrumental in the review of its project. Consequently, the review team's experience can be very different than the experience of the company's team, which can lead to conflict (because common ground cannot be found to effectively communicate) or a better drug development program than expected (the review team's perspective is so different that it helps bring new experience and ways of thinking to the regulatory team). How does the RI professional ensure the smoothest communication path forward for the company's team? The RI professional should gather as much information about the FDA review team as possible to understand each team member's educational background and perspective.

## What information should be collected?

The RI professional should collect the following information when reviewing the backgrounds of review team members:
- curricula vitae (education, work history)
- areas of special interest
- focus of research
- publications
- filings worked on for FDA (or other agency)
- tenure at agency

- questions asked during reviews and particular areas of concern found during reviews

## Where can reviewers' names be found—internally?

Reviewers' names and information can be culled from:

- meeting confirmation letters—the meeting confirmation letter from the agency will include a list of meeting attendees
- Pre-IND Meeting minutes from the agency will list the names of the attendees and potential IND reviewers
- IND Discipline Review letters—these letters sometimes include the name of the team member asking the questions
- For an IND or NDA review, it is possible to ask the Project Manager or Consumer Safety Officer directly for a list of all people working on an IND review team; this is subject to change over the life of the IND, so this information should be updated annually

## Where can background information be found?

LinkedIn is a valuable resource for this information. Also, the curricula vitae of FDA employees who have part-time professorships at academic institutions or previously were employed at academic institutions can be found on FDA's website or via Google.

## Where can INDs and NDAs previously worked on by reviewers be found?

PharmaPendium, the for-fee RI tool, can search through all NDA filings and find the reviewers' names quickly. From this, it is possible to find the filings on which particular reviewers worked and look at the individual reviews to understand the typical questions asked and understand whether there is a theme.

A general search of the FDA website or a Google search also can help provide the previous filings. If this search does not yield the desired results, a review of competitor Summary Bases of Approvals, specifically the list of reviewers, if posted, or if that is not available (and it will not be prior to 2008), a search through the specific discipline review for competitor drugs or other drugs in the therapeutic class, will garner reviewer names but will take much longer. After the drugs of interest have been identified, it is necessary to cull the identified reviews for the products on which the reviewer worked, the types of questions asked and information requested during the reviews. The reviewer's responsibility in each review versus his or her role in previous reviews also should be noted.

## Where are areas of special interest found?

PubMed (www.ncbi.nlm.nih.gov/pubmed) or a literature review by the reviewer's name can find publications. The publications should be examined to identify trends or themes in the literature.

## How should information be presented to the regulatory team?

**Table 10-1** illustrates how to collect and track the needed information. However, when presenting to a team, the RI professional should start with the reviewer's name, discipline, years at the agency, products reviewed and his or her typical areas of interest; keep the presentation at a high level.

**Table 9-1. Profile Collection Example**

| Name | Title | Education | Tenure at Agency/Other Positions of Note | Drugs Reviewed Positions on Previous Reviews/Drugs Reviewed |
|---|---|---|---|---|
| John Smith, MD | Medical Reviewer | 1999–2000 Transplant Fellow at Penn Johns Hopkins for research training | | Has extensive liver, kidney transplant experience and publications that include CsA use.<br><br>*21,560 and 21,628 for Certican® (not yet approved)* |
| Maisy Wong, PharmD | Medical Team Leader | BS in pharmacy, University of Wisconsin-Madison in 1991<br><br>PharmD and General Practice Residency at the University of Washington in Seattle in 1993<br><br>Three-year infectious disease research fellowship at the University of Illinois in Chicago (UIC) | 11 years First, as a clinical pharmacologist reviewing Phase 1 pharmacokinetic data, then Phase 2 and 3 safety and efficacy data as a clinical reviewer, and most recently as a secondary reviewer and supervisor of medical officers as an acting medical team leader<br><br>Presents frequently at Advisory Committee Meetings | Joined Division of Special Pathogen and Transplant Products (DSPTP) in 1998.<br><br>Specialized in Helicobacter pylori infections and completed multiple projects from *in vitro* microbiology studies to clinical trials.<br>INDs and NDAs for a wide range of antimicrobial products, including antibacterial, antifungal and antiparasitic products, and transplant immunosuppressants, in various capacities<br>19-537/S-049, ciprofloxacin tablets<br>20-780/S-013, ciprofloxacin oral suspension<br>19-847/S-027, ciprofloxacin IV 10 mg/mL<br>19-857/S-031, ciprofloxacin IV 5% dextrose<br>• Pediatric indication added for UTIs, no other quinolone had been approved for pediatric use except for anthrax exposure due to arthropathy.<br>• Recommended that Cipro only be used when other drugs have failed due to arthropathy in pediatric patients.<br>• All pediatric patients are required to be followed up for five years post treatment in observational study.<br>• Filed NDA Supplement with interim data.<br><br>Novartis NDA 22-268/ COARTEM<br>• Development of the program done completely outside the US—no input on protocols.<br><br>NDA 21-266 voriconazole tablets<br>NDA 21-267 voriconazole for injection |

| Name | Title | Education | Tenure at Agency/Other Positions of Note | Drugs Reviewed Positions on Previous Reviews/Drugs Reviewed |
|---|---|---|---|---|
| Ron Williams, PhD | Clinical Pharmacology | • **Medical University of South Carolina** PhD, Pharmaceutical Sciences, 1995–99 | • Regulatory Scientist FDA July 2002–Present (7 years 6 months)<br><br>• Senior Scientist Globomax LLC (now ICON US) March 2001–July 2002 (1 year 5 months)<br><br>• Staff Scientist Genzyme Corporation June 1999–March 2001 (1 year 10 months) | 19-537/S-049, ciprofloxacin tablets 20-780/S-013, ciprofloxacin oral suspension 19-847/S-027, ciprofloxacin IV 10 mg/mL 19-857/S-031, ciprofloxacin IV 5% dextrose<br>• The applicant used body weight as a covariate with an allometric exponent of 0.75 for clearance parameters based on literature. Instead of this, the applicant should have estimated the allometric exponent, which would have ensured correct estimation of the effect of body weight on clearance.<br>• The applicant used a base model comprising body weight as a covariate. Several covariates such as age were tested using this base model. This approach is not optimal, since age and body weight are interrelated; using a base model with body weight fails to distinguish the effect of age on clearance. Instead, the applicant should have tested the effect of age on the base model without body weight.<br><br>Novartis NDA 22-268/ COARTEM<br><br>NDA 21-530/20-938—Mobic (meloxicam)<br><br>NDA 21-227 Cancidas (IV Infusion) |
| Rishi Patel, PharmD, PhD | Clinical Pharmacology Team Leader | | Since 1998<br><br>In 1995, worked for South Florida Bioavailability Clinic Inc., Miami, FL; Pfizer Central Research, Groton, CT; and Marion Merrell Dow Inc., Kansas City, MO | 19-537/S-049, ciprofloxacin tablets 20-780/S-013, ciprofloxacin oral suspension 19-847/S-027, ciprofloxacin IV 10 mg/mL 19-857/S-031, ciprofloxacin IV 5% dextrose<br>• He reviewed and concurred with Dakshina Chilukuri, PhD finding above (was his supervisor)<br><br>Rapamune 21-110/21-083 (SE5-019)—Team Leader<br>• Wanted detailed listing of all batches used in individual studies.<br>• Asked in a postmarketing commitment for the establishment of an optimum therapeutic concentration range.<br>• Asked that a study on ethnicity as it pertains to PK be done (postmarketing).<br><br>Novartis NDA 22-268/COARTEM<br><br>NDA 21-266 voriconazole tablets NDA 21-267 voriconazole for injection<br><br>NDA 21-227 Cancidas<br><br>NDA: 20-634 S043 (Tablets); 20-635 S046 (Injection); 21-721 S011 (Oral Solution) Levaquin |

| Name | Title | Education | Tenure at Agency/Other Positions of Note | Drugs Reviewed Positions on Previous Reviews/Drugs Reviewed |
|---|---|---|---|---|
| Mark Brown, PhD | Pharmacology/ Toxicology Team Leader | | | **Novartis NDA 22-268/COARTEM**<br>• Supervisory role only.<br>• Recommendation for a juvenile toxicology study of Coartemether in dogs.<br>• Recommendation that the applicant conduct an intramuscular neurotoxicity study of artemether in beagle dogs to assess whether neurologic deterioration occurs following discontinuation of drug (modified recommendation after Advisory Committee Meeting).<br>• Recommend bacterial mutagenicity assays (i.e., Ames assays) for particular artemether degradants and lumefantrine process impurities, which have structural alerts for genetic toxicity. |
| Carla Fahey, PhD | Chemistry Reviewer | 1979, Wake Forest, North Carolina | Since at least 1999 | **Restatsis** (http://www.accessdata.fda.gov/drugsatfda_docs/nda/2003/21-023_Restasis_Admindoc.PDF—Not a lead reviewer, just helped out on a teleconference<br><br>**Rapamunne 21-083/21-110**<br>• Requested label and carton changes and samples of the drug product container closure systems (these had to be sent twice).<br>• Requested additional data to support requested 24 month stability.<br>• Very detailed feedback on postapproval stability plan including fourth year timepoint, and accelerated testing was a separate protocol.<br>• Two FDA labs were used to confirm the methods validation used<br>• Requested new dissolution specifications for postapproval stability.<br>• Very active in review.<br><br>**Everolimus 22-334**<br>• A recent inspection of Novartis Pharma AG, Basel, identified a deficiency in the validation of HPLC Method 30001.01, Determination of Related Substances in the Drug Substance. Apparently the method was not completely validated with respect to the determination of impurity (late 2008). |

| Name | Title | Education | Tenure at Agency/Other Positions of Note | Drugs Reviewed Positions on Previous Reviews/Drugs Reviewed |
|------|-------|-----------|------------------------------------------|--------------------------------------------------------------|
| Karen Harder, ScD | Statistical Reviewer | | Since at least 2004 | 19-537/S-049, ciprofloxacin tablets 20-780/S-013, ciprofloxacin oral suspension 19-847/S-027, ciprofloxacin IV 10 mg/mL 19-857/S-031, ciprofloxacin IV 5% dextrose • Nothing vastly different from the sponsor's findings.<br><br>Rapamune/SIROLIMUS/NDA 21-083— Team Leader Significantly higher rate of discontinuation in a CsA control arm was a concern. Sponsor was asked to explore impact and whether it affected the safety conclusions and introduced bias.<br><br>Novartis NDA 22-268/COARTEM • The interpretation of results is limited by the fact that they were single center studies, both performed at the same site in China.<br><br>NDA 21-266 voriconazole tablets NDA 21-267 voriconazole for injection |

# CHAPTER 10

# Inspection Tracking and Inspector Profiles

## Inspections

Health authorities inspect establishments that manufacture, process, pack or hold regulated products, to determine whether they are in compliance with regulations. Upon completing the inspection, if objectionable conditions are observed, the health authority provides the owner of the establishment with a document that typically includes the name of the firm and the date(s) of inspection, and lists the observations made by the investigator during the inspection. Countries with transparency laws often post these inspection findings on their websites.

Typically, the RI professional wants to review the inspection and compliance history of vendors or sites that will be working with the company. If an Establishment Inspection Report (EIR) or Warning Letter has been issued, or the investigator is on the disqualification or debarment list, it would be beneficial to have that information before working with the vendor, and the RI professional can be called upon to provide this data.

Another reason to track inspection findings is to help the company's manufacturing or clinical sites track inspection trends. Even though FDA (www.fda.gov/ICECI/Inspections/default.htm) and

other health authorities publish compliance and inspection guides, there are trends or themes that develop over the years. The RI professional should ensure the company is aware of these, taking them into account and preparing for them in upcoming audits. One way to do this is to review Warning Letters on a yearly basis, looking for trends in all countries where the information is available and the company has manufacturing plants.

## Good Clinical Practice

Good Clinical Practice (GCP) is an international ethical and scientific quality standard for designing, conducting, recording and reporting trials involving the participation of human subjects as published by the International Conference on Harmonisation (ICH). Compliance with this standard provides public assurance that trial subjects' rights, safety and wellbeing are protected, consistent with the principles in the *Declaration of Helsinki*, and that clinical trial data are credible.

## Good Manufacturing Practice

Current Good Manufacturing Practice (CGMP) regulations are enforced by

ICH-observing countries. CGMPs require systems that assure proper design, monitoring and control of manufacturing processes and facilities. Adherence to CGMP regulations assures the identity, strength, quality, stability and purity of drug products by requiring manufacturers to control manufacturing operations adequately. This includes establishing strong quality management systems, obtaining appropriate quality raw materials, establishing robust operating procedures, detecting and investigating product quality deviations and maintaining reliable testing laboratories. This formal system of controls, if put into practice properly by a pharmaceutical company, helps prevent contamination, mix-ups, deviations, failures and errors. This ensures drug products meet their quality standards.

## Good Laboratory Practice

Good Laboratory Practice (GLP) regulations govern the conduct of nonclinical safety studies and *in vitro* studies. The importance of nonclinical laboratory studies requires them to be conducted according to scientifically sound protocols and with meticulous attention to quality and documentation of all study procedures.

## Databases to Find Inspection Data

When asked to monitor trends or to look at particular sites or investigators, the first step in finding inspection data is to know where to look for it on FDA's website or that of any other health authority. Different authorities provide listings, spreadsheets or databases to mine for the data needed.

### GCP

If an inspection was conducted on a potential IRB or clinical site, but there was no associated Warning Letter, Untitled Letter, or other information available, the outcome letter can be requested from the site or the health authority via the *Freedom of Information Act* (*FOIA*) or Right to Information (RTI) (See Chapter 7).

To ensure the company's clinical sites maintain compliance, an annual review should be conducted for all sites, looking for the names of investigators on a variety of clinical lists (if this is not done, the company might accidently sign up an investigator who is debarred or disqualified, which can have a major impact on a marketing application).

Bioresearch Monitoring (BIMO) conducts all GCP inspections that cover:
- Institutional Review Board
- Radioactive Drug Research Committee
- sponsors, contract research organizations and monitors
- clinical investigators

**Additional Databases**
- inspections database www.fda.gov/ICECI/EnforcementActions/ucm222557.htm
- Warning Letters www.fda.gov/ICECI/EnforcementActions/WarningLetters/default.htm
- clinical debarment list (those who can never participate in clinical research again) www.fda.gov/ICECI/EnforcementActions/FDADebarmentList/default.htm
- clinical investigators disqualification proceedings (for those who can eventually participate in clinical research again) www.fda.gov/ICECI/EnforcementActions/ucm321308.htm and the database at: www.accessdata.fda.gov/scripts/SDA/sdNavigation.cfm?sd=clinicalinvestigatorsdisqualificationproceedings&previewMode=true&displayAll=true
- administrative actions (for those who can participate in clinical research under supervision) ori.hhs.gov/misconduct/AdminBulletinBoard.shtml

### GLP

To find GLP laboratory inspection information and to learn whether a particular laboratory has any findings that need to be considered and

**Table 10-1. Example of GMP Trends**

| No. | Sponsor | Warning Letter Reference ID | Subpart B—Organization and Personnel | | | | Subpart—Building and Facilities | | | | | | |
|---|---|---|---|---|---|---|---|---|---|---|---|---|---|
| | | | 211.22 | 211.25 | 211.28 | 211.34 | 211.42 | 211.44 | 211.46 | 211.48 | 211.50 | 211.52 | 211.56 |
| 1 | ACS Dobfar | WL:320-05-03 | | | | X | ( c) | X | | X | | X | |
| 2 | ABC Pharma | | | | | | | | | | | | |
| 3 | KPT Pharma | | | X | | X | | | X | | | X | |

reviewed during the company's audit go to www.fda.gov/ICECI/EnforcementActions/BioresearchMonitoring/NonclinicalLaboratoriesInspectedunderGoodLaboratoryPractices/ucm2005399.htm.

BIMO also conducts the following GLP inspections:

- Good Laboratory Practice (Nonclinical Laboratories)
- Good Laboratory Practice Program (Nonclinical Laboratories) EPA Data Audit Inspections

## GMP

FDA inspects pharmaceutical manufacturing facilities worldwide using scientifically and CGMP-trained individuals whose job is to evaluate whether a company is following the CGMP regulations. FDA also relies on reports of potentially defective drug products from the public and industry. The agency often will use these reports to identify sites for which an inspection or investigation is needed. Following are resources to help track GMP status of companies:

- Warning Letters www.fda.gov/ICECI/EnforcementActions/WarningLetters/default.htm
- EIRs www.fda.gov/AboutFDA/CentersOffices/OfficeofGlobalRegulatoryOperationsandPolicy/ORA/ORAElectronicReadingRoom/default.htm (If the EIR is not yet posted on the FDA website, it will need to be requested via FOI, see Chapter 7.)
- annual list of inspections (2014) www.fda.gov/downloads/regulatoryinformation/legislation/federalfooddrugandcosmeticactfdcact/significantamendmentstothefdcact/fdasia/ucm384063.pdf
- annual listing of inspection findings or trends (output is similar to **Table 10-1** but not company specific) www.fda.gov/ICECI/EnforcementActions/ucm381526.htm
- inspections database (output is similar to **Table 10-1,** but no specific infractions are given): www.fda.gov/ICECI/EnforcementActions/ucm222557.htm
- inspection citations (more like **Table 10-1,** but drug or biologic information will need to be separated from all other types of citations such as food, cosmetics, dietary supplements and medical devices) www.fda.gov/ICECI/EnforcementActions/ucm346077.htm

Typically, searching the last five years will help establish trends over time, and this can be updated when a new list is published or a Warning Letter is issued.

## Cooperative Agreements

The Pharmaceutical Inspection Co-operation Scheme (PIC/S) was established in 1995 as an extension to the Pharmaceutical Inspection Convention (PIC) of 1970. PIC/S is an informal cooperative arrangement between regulatory authorities in the field of GMP of medicinal products for human or veterinary use. It is open to any authority having a comparable GMP inspection system.

PIC/S comprises participating authorities mainly from Europe but also from Africa (e.g., South Africa), the Americas (e.g., Argentina and Canada), Asia (e.g., Malaysia and Singapore) and Australasia (e.g., Australia). The list of PIC/S participating authorities is available at www.picscheme.org.

PIC/S aims at harmonizing inspection procedures worldwide by developing common standards in the GMP field and providing training opportunities for inspectors. It also aims at facilitating cooperation and networking between competent authorities, regional and international organizations, thus increasing mutual confidence.

PIC/S's GMP publication is available at www.picscheme.org/publication.php?id=4.

### Memoranda of Understanding

Additionally, like PIC/S, FDA, EMA and Canada have entered into agreements with foreign governments regarding the quality of foods, drugs and other products exported. A list of all MOUs between FDA and ex-US countries can be found at www.fda.gov/InternationalPrograms/Agreements/MemorandaofUnderstanding/default.htm.

EU Mutual Recognition Agreements are available at www.ema.europa.eu/ema/index.jsp?curl=pages/regulation/document_listing/document_listing_000248.jsp&mid=WC0b01ac058005f8ac.

### Ex-US Inspection Data Information

Typically, data are required for more than just the US. Some additional resources are:
- EMA inspections www.ema.europa.eu/ema/index.jsp?curl=pages/regulation/general/general_content_000161.jsp&mid=WC0b01ac0580024592
- EMA GLP inspections www.ema.europa.eu/ema/index.jsp?curl=pages/regulation/general/glp_compliance.jsp
- EMA GCP inspections www.ema.europa.eu/ema/index.jsp?curl=pages/regulation/general/general_content_000072.jsp&mid=WC0b01ac05800268ad
- EudraGMDP is the European Community database of manufacturing authorizations and certificates of GMP eudragmp.ema.europa.eu and http://eudragmdp.ema.europa.eu/inspections/displayWelcome.do contains the following information:
  o manufacturing and import authorizations
  o GMP certificates
  o statements of noncompliance with GMP
  o GMP inspection planning in third countries
- Health Canada GMP inspection reports www.hc-sc.gc.ca/dhp-mps/compli-conform/gmp-bpf/2011-03-31-report-rapport-eng.php
- Health Canada Inspection Policy www.hc-sc.gc.ca/dhp-mps/compli-conform/gmp-bpf/pol/pol_0011_insp_drug_ltr-doc-eng.php#a53conform/gmp-bpf/pol/pol_0011_insp_drug_ltr-doc-eng.php#a53
- Australian Therapeutic Goods Administration (TGA), inspection basics:
  o www.tga.gov.au/industry/manuf-inspections-frequency.htm#.Uv68j3bTmP8
  o www.tga.gov.au/industry/manuf-inspections-overview.htm#.Uv6863bTmP8
  o www.tga.gov.au/industry/manuf-compliance-history.htm#.Uv69LXbTmP8

### World Health Organization

The World Health Organization Public Inspection Reports (WHOPIR) summarize the inspection reports of:
- active pharmaceutical ingredient (API) manufacturing sites

- finished product (FP) manufacturing sites
- facilities, such as contract research organizations (CROs), where a bioequivalence study or other clinical study was performed
- quality control laboratories

The WHOPIR reflects the inspection report and gives a summary of the observations and findings made during the inspection but excludes confidential proprietary information. It also indicates the date and duration of the inspection as well as the scope of the inspection. Inspection reports are included at apps.who.int/ prequal/WHOPIR/pq_whopir.htm.

### How do you compile the information in a meaningful way?

How data are presented really depends on the audience. The presentation found at www.pda.org/Chapters/North-America-cont/New-England/Presentations/ Inspection-Trends.aspx gives a line listing of the trends found by year for GMP inspections. This is a great way to present the final data, but how should the information initially be captured? **Table 10-1** is a sample Excel table used to capture all initial trend data.

## What inspectors should be profiled?

The RI professional should only profile inspectors who are relevant to the company and the products it produces or clinical sites it uses. Efforts should concentrate on the inspectors who inspect:

- manufacturing sites (in use or may be used)
- clinical sites (in use or may be used)
- CROs or other vendors (in use or may be used)
- sponsors

## Inspector profiles—what to collect?

The following information should be collected when reviewing inspectors'

backgrounds, by discipline (GMP, GCP, GLP):

- curricula vitae (education, work history)
- number of years with the agency
- areas of special interest; typical topics
- typical questions asked (if available) and typical findings

## Where can inspector information be found?

Unless the company has an RI database that has compiled this information already, it will be necessary to search for it. These data are time consuming to find but can be mined using the following sources:

- general web search of inspector's name
- key word search of inspector's name on the health authority website
- manual search of all Warning and Untitled Letters and EIRs, looking for the inspector's name and infractions noted

## Why is this Information Important?

Everyone has a bias, even if they do not like to admit it. The RI professional wants to find the inspectors' personal biases, so the company can prepare and anticipate inspector questions and data requests that might be different from those of other reviewers, and cross-reference this to the GMP, GCP and GLP annual findings to look for trends.

If the company knows the inspectors and the annual trends, it will be better prepared for inspections or re-inspection (assuming all deficiencies have been corrected).

**References**
**US Inspections, Compliance, Enforcement, and Criminal Investigations** http://www.fda.gov/ ICECI/Inspections/default.htm

CHAPTER 11

# Additional RI Operations Responsibilities

Besides researching a question or conducting surveillance, regulatory intelligence operations can provide additional services including, but not limited to:

- newsletters
- targeted alerts
- training
- regulatory trends, hot topics

## Newsletters

The type of newsletter a company produces depends on its customers and their needs. Some customers want an update on new official regulatory documents. Others prefer a detailed analysis of official regulatory documents, pertinent meetings, new product approvals and the impact of these on the company.

The newsletter format and schedule for dispersal also vary. A newsletter can be as simple as a daily, weekly or monthly email with links, a "What's New" section on an intranet site, or a highly stylized, published document. If a company does not have time to write a newsletter, it can use an RI database or hire an outside vendor to produce one.

To understand whether customers are actually using the newsletters and whether this is a worthy investment,

software is available to track how many people have opened and used the newsletter on an ongoing basis.

## Target Alerts

This is a "mini newsletter" (instead of a mass mailing) that is directed at a very specific target group within the company that would like to know about any changes in predefined topics of interest rapidly so they can be constantly current on the topic. The alert can be cut and pasted links, a summary with links or an in-depth analysis of the topic and the changes; however it is usually an email with a note and a link letting the person or group know about the change.

## Training

The RI group is the company's eyes and ears with respect to changes in the regulatory landscape, upcoming paradigm shifts and what the company will need to know to keep abreast of regulatory compliance issues to stay competitive.

When new regulations or guidance documents are published, the RI department typically reads them first and disseminates the important points to stakeholders. Sometimes, however, because the impact is on the overall company, and SOPs will be affected, company-wide training can be provided. This can be done through QA (if SOPs are involved) or RI if the impact is more informative (or through RI if company-wide, but QA will need to be involved to document training or update to an SOP).

Sometimes the RI department conducts "Lunch and Learns" and provides a presentation of a "hot topic" during the lunch hour.

The RI group also can be a repository for all training materials received from meetings attended by employees to create a training library. When facing a new challenge, it is always easiest to review what has been done previously or has been suggested by an expert and a training library can provide this resource.

Often regulators will present concepts behind a new paradigm or initiative at professional meetings, such as those offered by DIA and RAPS. An example of this was the Target Product Profile in 2005–06; FDA presented this concept at the annual DIA conference, asking for industry input well before the concept paper was available on the agency's website. If an RI department member had attended this meeting, he or she could have presented the concept after the meeting to help shape internal company policy and be better prepared when the guidance document was issued.

## Regulatory Trends; Hot Topics

How is something deemed a "hot topic?" It depends on the company's perspective and product line but, typically, a "hot topic" is a tragedy or significant public health safety issue to which FDA is reacting that inspires further regulation, or a topic being debated in the press and by the regulators.

It also might be draft guidance or regulations issued for comment, or the issuance of a final regulation or guidance that garners a strong reaction from the press or industry. A hot topic becomes obvious by the number of times it is mentioned or covered in a variety of press outlets over an extended period of time; items that get one or two mentions typically are not hot topics unless the impact to a specific company is significant.

A hot topic might be internal to a company if all the development teams seem to be talking about something like how to start clinical trials or put together marketing applications in a variety of countries and how the information compares. Another topic could be how the *Orphan Drug Act* works, its benefits and what countries have similar legislation. It might seem very obvious to the regulatory department because it deals with this information regularly, but external to the regulatory department, this is an unfamiliar topic.

Another source of a hot topic can be pending or recently approved legislation, such as a reauthorization of the *Prescription Drug User Fee Act (PDUFA)*. Once the bill becomes law, it is prudent for the RI department to analyze the impact it would have on the company, industry or pipeline and to ensure management is aware of the implications.

A hot topic summary can be purchased from vendors or consultants or put together as a research question and posted on the company's intranet site.

# 12

# Regulatory Strategy

## What is Strategy?

The *Merriam-Webster Medical Dictionary* (2002) defines "strategy" as "an adaptation or complex of adaptations (as of behavior, metabolism, or structure) that serves or appears to serve an important function in achieving evolutionary success." Therefore, regulatory strategy could be seen as the adaptations a company makes to move its product from development to marketing approval.

Regulatory strategy incorporates the drug development plan, outstanding issues or questions, background information, regulations and/or guidance documents, strategic advice, past precedents (if any) clinical endpoints, nonclinial plan, stability plan and recommendations on implementation. Additionally, strategy can take the form of or include:

- an individual question as it pertains to a development program or a change in regulations
- a review of the development plan (gap analysis)
- a drug development plan (US, EU or global)
- therapeutic area analysis
- competitor pipeline analysis
- development risks
- commercial planning
- lifecycle analysis

Strategy relates to the whole development program, so unexpected issues can be identified prospectively, not randomly appear. This means considering CMC, nonclinical, clinical and regulatory at all times and how they are interwoven and the impact they have on each other.

This chapter explores the requirements for developing a strategy for a US-centric drug development plan with some global considerations added as well, since drug development is increasingly global.

## Why implement a strategy?

As the old adage says, "If you don't plan, then you plan to fail." Implementing a strategy allows the company to map a path forward and examine the pitfalls and mitigate any risks, challenges or issues the drug might face. Companies tend to plan to fail by not recognizing the value of strategic planning. They may claim to be "too busy" to put together an overall strategic plan. Putting together a Target Product Profile (TPP) or draft package insert at the end of Phase 2 or during NDA preparation, only to find additional nonclinical or clinical studies (such as QT prolongation) need to be conducted to support the filing or claims, is not a winning strategy. The company should plan early and look at all its options before proceeding with the program. In the long run, developing a strategy will save time and money and focus the development team. This chapter provides an overview of the when, who, what and why of regulatory strategy (in the form of a drug development plan with some package insert elements) and FDA's perspective on the company's strategy or lack thereof. Benefits of a strategy include:

- drives identification and management of prospectively defined regulatory issues or unexpected requirements (e.g., an excipient not being approved for use in all countries)
- identifies and mitigates risk in the development program
- documents the strategic decision-making process and input from all team members
- serves as the framework for evaluating change
- creates awareness of key project issues and risks within the development and management team
- ensures efficient utilization of project resources
- can create credibility with regulatory agencies because the company has planned the whole program carefully
- can result in a timely approval for a product, thereby meeting business objectives
- expedites patient access to new and improved products and therapies

## When to Implement a Strategy

The ideal time to construct a strategy is at the pre-IND stage, to get the team thinking about all the elements of the drug development plan. Pre-IND meeting requirements include submission of a development plan with the meeting package; this item can drive the team to map out a plan (however, please note the meeting package will not be rejected if it is not included). Additionally, if the company communicates the strategy to FDA via a TPP or by other means (typically in a meeting), this informs the agency of the company's strategic thinking.

## Who

Typically, the global development team works together to create the drug development plan. The effort is led by a regulatory director or vice president who drafts a plan for team discussion. Each team member brings his or her unique perspective to the process and affects the ultimate outcome of the strategy negotiations, which in turn influences the drug development process. The team members and their typical simplified questions and/or perspectives about any new compound are shown in **Table 12-1**.

Putting together the drug development plan requires all perspectives to be aligned toward the same goal, and each team member's needs to be addressed, which can be difficult since viewpoints can diverge.

## What should a strategy document look like?

The strategy document format depends on the company, its culture, the past experience of regulatory professionals who are leading the effort and the amount of detail to be included in the final product. Ultimately, a strategy document is an organized meld of all the facets of drug development from pre-IND through NDA and into commercialization on which multiple stakeholders have agreed. Whether the document is an Excel spreadsheet or a working "book," it must capture and document any changes to the drug development process so the whole team understands them and their impact on the strategy. The strategic output should include:

- development assumptions for Phases 1–3 and commercial for

**Table 12-1. Contributions by Discipline for Strategy Development**

| Member | Perspective/Questions |
|---|---|
| Preclinical scientist | • Is there a scientific basis or rationale for this drug?<br>• Does this rationale justify moving into humans?<br>• Do pharmacology studies demonstrate the mechanism of action?<br>• Are findings reproducible?<br>• Any specific toxicology signals of concern?<br>• What battery of nonclinical studies will need to be conducted for an approvable NDA? |
| Manufacturing Representative | • Can the API be made consistently, and where will the source materials be obtained?<br>• Can the compound be manufactured consistently and at current facilities?<br>• Will outside vendors or contract manufacturers be needed?<br>• How much will it cost to make?<br>• Is the formulation correct?<br>• Is the drug stable?<br>• Will any methods have to be developed?<br>• What container closure method will be used? |
| Regulatory Affairs Director | • What is the regulatory status of the drug?<br>• Has it been approved before in the current form or another?<br>• Can precedents be relied upon, or are they too old?<br>• What regulations or guidance documents apply?<br>• What FDA division will review the drug?<br>• What pathway should be chosen based on the pathways laid by precedent drugs, or is there no precedent? |
| Legal Department Representative | • Can we protect our intellectual property, or is it infringing on others'?<br>• Is it patentable? |
| Medical Director | • Is there a medical need or therapeutic value for the drug?<br>• How is the disease currently diagnosed and treated?<br>• What is the standard of care for the disease, and how will it be impacted by the new drug?<br>• What drugs are used off label to treat this disease?<br>• What are the concomitant medications?<br>• Can we prove safety and efficacy?<br>• How will the trial be designed, and what endpoints will be used?<br>• How many patients are in the target population?<br>• How many studies will be needed for an approvable NDA? |
| Finance Representative/ Business Development | • What is the return on investment?<br>• How much will it cost to develop?<br>• Can we afford this development program on our own, do we need to raise capital to complete or should we find a partner? |
| Marketing Representative | • What is the new drug's potential market position?<br>• What are the other drugs on the market, and what are their annual sales?<br>• How is the new drug different than others, and is there room for a new therapy on the market?<br>• What will someone be willing to pay for the drug? |
| Reimbursement Specialist | • What metrics need to be included in the studies to justify the price of the drug?<br>• Will there be reimbursement issues with any payers? |

clinical, quality (CMC) and non-clinical disciplines
- answers to development questions and issues, by phase and discipline (subject to change), using multiple tools
- exploration of accelerated approval options
- information on product exclusivity
- documented risks, based on assumptions
- plan for timing FDA interactions
- questions arising, by phase of development, to address with the agency
- clinical endpoints and indication information
- history of the molecule (including FDA actions and past precedents)

**Figure 12-1. High-Level Strategy Output**

| Indication | Treatment of Type 2 Diabetes (prevention would be too large a trial) |
|---|---|
| **Endpoints (Primary + Secondary)** | • HbA1c*<br>• Daily glycemic control*<br>*based on guidance document recommendation |
| **FDA Division** | DMEP |
| **Division Challenges** | • Rigid and strict with regulatory requirements, "box checkers;" Congress has called its actions into question<br>• Need to follow the prescribed development plan and not stray from it; tends not to grant alternative regulatory science approaches<br>• It has too many customers and not enough time or resources |
| **Alternatives** | • A variety of standard of care treatments |
| **Advantages** | • General label<br>• Well-defined path forward for endpoints |
| **Disadvantages** | • Higher regulatory hurdles with current division for Phase 3 trials<br>• More competition in marketplace for conducting clinical trials and market share<br>• Clinical trials are expensive and need to go ex-US for study sites<br>• Many treatment modalities available<br>• Patient population is not compliant with multiple co-morbidities |
| **Phase 1 Trial(s)** | Healthy volunteers; approximately 100 patients |
| **Phase 2 Trial** | Phase 2 Dosing and Efficacy Trial (not longer than three months) in 200–500 patients; randomized and placebo controlled |
| **Phase 3 Trial** | 2,000+ patients, 1,000 in each Phase 3 or 2,000 in a single trial with a longer term extension trial. Recently approved drugs include almost 10,000+ patients in their safety database.<br>• Randomized and placebo-controlled monotherapy (less than six months in duration)<br>• Randomized and placebo-controlled add-on therapy (less than six months in duration)<br>• Randomized, active control<br>• QT prolongation and liver toxicology sub-studies will need to be conducted<br>*estimation based on guidance documents |
| **Prevalence** | 25.6 million people in the US have diabetes (diagnosed or undiagnosed) http://diabetes.niddk.nih.gov/dm/pubs/statistics/#Estimation |
| **Safety Database** | 2,500 patients with long-term data at time of NDA filing (six months, one year and some at two years) |
| **Barriers to Proceed: Studies and Question That Need to be Addressed** | **Clinical Study Three months or longer**<br>• Repeat dose toxicology studies (rodent and non-rodent) conducted for over three months<br>• Segment 1 and 2 repro tox studies<br><br>**Clinical Study Six months or longer**<br>• Two-year carcinogenicity study in rates (or six month rat transgenic model with approval from CAC [CAC review and approval can take three to four months]) |

• creating the TPP/initial label
• creating and mapping goals in a timeline

See **Figure 12-1** for a high-level strategy summary.

## Playbook Format

This is a comprehensive document outlining all the components of a regulatory strategy:

• It outlines all the assumptions, regulatory filings and timeline.
• It captures the strategy at a point in time:

- o Sections can be added or deleted as needed.
- o It can be updated as assumptions change.
- The most important section of the document is the TPP.

## Goals

- For clinical programs, this section should identify the product-specific target disease and patient population from the commercial plan, i.e., target indication or target label claim.
- For early programs, a single target disease may not have been selected. In this case, the focus should be on goals for current stage, e.g., nonclinical program, diseases being considered for an initial target, etc. For approved programs, provide lifecycle management goal(s).
- This section also should identify major CMC goals for the current program stage, e.g., new product registration, new formulation, significant manufacturing process change.

## Regulatory Assumptions

The goal of this section is to clarify whether the path to registration for the target disease and patient population (indication) is straightforward (guidelines available, precedents set, program-specific agreements with health authorities) or will require more specific negotiation with health authorities (no guidelines or recent drug approvals, no validated clinical endpoints, new class of drug, no drug approved for indication). The following should be considered:

- availability of ICH, US, EU or other country guidelines for each indication, nonclinical study requirements or CMC; significant differences should be highlighted
- program-specific advice received from health authorities (if any)

- IND/CTA study start-up documents, timelines, activities and support needed
- clarity of clinical endpoints for regulatory approval and regional differences
- route to approval for competitive drugs; issues encountered by other drugs
- status of relevant global regulatory issues, e.g., Transmissible Spongiform Encephalopathy (TSE)/Bovine Spongiform Encephalopathy (BSE)

## Filing Assumptions

This section should provide a brief general overview of the plans for filing for clinical trial initiation and marketing application approval, including the timeline, the agency review timeline and the type of review in each specific country in which clinical trial and marketing applications will be filed:

- indicate eligibility for special filing mechanisms, such as orphan drug, fast track, priority review, accelerated approval, breakthrough therapy, etc.
- detail should be appropriate to each country's development stage and application-specific requirements
- early in development, emphasis should be on clinical trial applications, pre-IND meetings, etc.
- Phase 2b and beyond will require more detail on marketing applications, including geographic regions where applications will be filed
- late in development, plans for filing in ex-US markets should be addressed

## Efficacy Assumptions

This section should list assumptions on regulatory requirements to achieve target indication:

- provide information on clinical trial design, endpoints and duration of treatment

- standard of care (SOC) for the indication in each country and how it affects global clinical trials
- number of patients needed to show a statistical difference in each indication, by trial and phase

## Safety Assumptions

This section should list assumptions about regulatory requirements to establish safety to support the TPP:

- size of safety database, need for studies in special populations, drug interactions and any product-specific attributes that impact safety data requirements
- how safety endpoints might differ in countries based on SOC and scientific advice feedback

## Nonclinical Assumptions

This section should list assumptions on regulatory requirements for nonclinical studies to support the TPP and individual country differences, when appropriate.

## CMC Assumptions

This section should list country-specific assumptions related to major CMC goals:

- in addition, CMC assumptions that impact the clinical plan, e.g., a significant manufacturing change may necessitate a bioequivalence or immunogenicity trial
- ability of the drug to comply with multiple compendial specifications
- whether excipients used are accepted or considered novel in each country must be determined
- country-specific stability requirements need to be determined
- timing of manufacturing campaigns to support Phase 1, 2 and 3 clinical studies; commercial lots for marketing application stability and process validation lots

## Labeling Assumptions

This section should list assumptions on the types of label statements supported by the current development plan:

- indicate differences in labeled indications expected by country and SOC
- insert TTP and competitive labeling here
- desired indications or text currently not supported by a planned study

## Risk Management Assessment

This section should include a table with the following headers:

- Risk Event
- Probability
- Impact
- Management Plan

Complete these subsections when risks are identified and a strategy is developed for mitigating those risks in the development program.

## Timeline

This section should present the timeline to approval, including, at least, the following activities, as appropriate:

- Pre-IND Meeting (if needed)
- IND/CTA filings
- End-of-Phase 2 Meetings/Planned EMA Scientific Advice
- Pre-NDA Meeting/EU Presubmission Meeting (Scientific Advice in other countries if needed)
- registration filing (five major markets, ex-US)
- regulatory approvals

## Other Items to Include:

- minutes from key meetings and teleconferences with health authorities
- regulatory guidelines—provide list of regulatory guidance documents, including FDA and CHMP guidelines, FDA Advisory Committee Meeting minutes, EPARs, etc.
- product exclusivity expected in each region

- patent status in each country in which a marketing application will be filed

## Where to start?

Typically, teams start with the draft label or the TPP and build on this for a playbook since this represents the first attempt at combining information from all disciplines. If this has not been developed yet, it can be pulled together after the playbook is drafted. The following content needs to be covered, but the compound and indication will drive the ultimate format of the strategy document:

- medical and commercial requirements (usually have key marketing messages that need to be woven into the NDA modules)
- patient requirements (indications and need for drug)
- research and development requirements
- adverse event profile
- regulatory requirements

A breakdown of the specific items usually researched and evaluated and the decisions made about each topic that affect drug development for the US or on a global basis follow.

### Assumptions

To create a strategy, especially if in Phase 0/1, some assumptions need to be made about the drug and the development process. In the early phases, only minimal information is available. These assumptions will provide the basis on which to build the strategy document. These assumptions should be documented so information changes can lead to strategy document adjustments. This documentation also helps to determine risks the program might face, based on assumptions and drug development issues, and allows the team to come up with solutions for these issues.

### Key Milestones to Include

This usually is used as a timeline for the project and should include each country in which a marketing application is planned:

- final toxicology study completed/draft study report is ready
- Pre-IND Meeting (if needed, but not required)
- IND submission + 30 days
- first patient dosed
- Phase 1 study
- End-of-Phase 1 Meeting
- Phase 2 study initiated
- End-of-Phase 2 Meeting
- Phase 3 study initiated
- last patient dosed in Phase 3
- Pre-NDA Meeting
- NDA submitted
  - o NDA accepted
  - o Preapproval Inspections
  - o clinical site inspections
  - o tradename acceptance
  - o REMS negotiations
  - o label negotiations
  - o NDA approved
- Drug marketed

### Indications and Claims

- target indications
  - o requirements for clinical trials by indication, which might differ by country
- label format, content (organization) and language requirements for each country
- competitor label analysis

### Disease or Condition

- prevalence
- diagnosis
- prognosis
- treatment options including standard of care
- adverse events expected for disease, expected for other drugs in class and for the disease itself
- off-label use
- in which countries and/or population does this disease typically occur

### Unmet Medical Need

- disease demographics
- description of current management of disease
- proposed therapies

### Regulatory

- health authority (reviewing division)
- regulatory hurdles
- regulatory submissions needed
- supporting documentation
- regulatory risks and mitigations
- meetings with regulatory authorities and Scientific Advice
- product classification
- drug class

### Country-Specific Approval Strategies

- approval route
- approval options (fast track, priority, accelerated approval, orphan, breakthrough therapy, etc.)
- marketing exclusivity expected
- in which countries should marketing applications be submitted and their documentation requirements

### Preclinical Testing Program

- relevant regulations and guidance
- pharmacology
- safety testing
- mechanism of action or mechanistic studies
- pharmacokinetics
- toxicology
- testing that can be conducted in Phase 2, Phase 3 or postapproval
- biocompatibility
- risks and mitigations
- waivers to be requested
- any previous or published data that can be relied upon

### Clinical

- clinical strategy that encompasses:
  - Phase 1, 2 and 3 studies
  - location of clinical trials
    - Ethics Committee approval timeframe
    - regulatory authority approval timeframe
    - core documents needed for trials
    - trial start up times
  - country-by-country diagnosis, treatment and SOC for disease
  - required safety database for a marketing application
- risk mitigation
- key opinion leaders in the field
- key publications for the disease
- publication planning

### Manufacturing

- components/ingredients of drug substance and product
- GMP status of all starting materials and final finished product
- compendial ingredients (by country)
- excipients and regulatory status
- Master/Site Files needed
- contract manufacturing needed or on-site manufacturing
- sterilization
- stability requirements (by country)
- packaging and labeling
- import/export issues
- clinical trial supplies and materials
- timing of process validation

### Commercial Strategy

- other products on the market and their market share
- clinical trials needed to establish noninferiority or superiority
- market need for new product and estimated annual earnings
- potential countries to market compound

### Competitive Information

- other companies with products for the same indication
  - stage of development

- clinical study details and
  study results
- competitor claims (label)
- recent launches, by country for
  each indication

*Reimbursement*

- for each country, requirements
  should be determined for:
  o patient-reported outcomes
  o pharmacoeconomics
  information
  o reimbursement of similar
  drugs in a variety of countries
  (to help develop price points)
  o data needed by insurance
  companies to establish
  reimbursement

*Intellectual Property*

- applicable patents and expirations
- country-specific patent law
  interpretation or whether patent protection exists in certain
  countries

*Miscellaneous*

- resources needed
- project milestones
- translations needed
- lifecycle management strategy

## What specific questions need to be addressed?

To create a strategy, it is necessary to have a thorough understanding of the development process. Creating a strategy begins by asking certain questions, which can help determine questions the agency may have when it meets with the company. The team should think about all the questions the agency might ask, so team members need to think like agency representatives when creating a strategy. This helps identify any potential concerns and allows the company to mitigate them at the appropriate development phase. This is not an exhaustive list of questions since every development program is unique (they can

be prospective or retrospective, depending on when the strategy is created).

## Why document a strategy?

As FDA has noted, "If it isn't documented, it doesn't exist." There are many reasons to document a strategy in a playbook for the team:

- The team members are being asked to think critically about all the factors that go into drug development, not just their small segments. By seeing the whole picture, people understand how their small portions fit into the overall strategy.
- A formal written analysis of the regulatory strategy provides a reference as to why a decision was made at a particular juncture in the development timeline, so new team members can understand the whole picture. In addition, it can serve as the foundation document for any future updates.
- When assumptions or some component in the strategy changes, their impact on other facets of the drug development program can be evaluated.

A playbook also:

- drives identification and management of prospectively defined regulatory issues (not learning about an unexpected problem later in the process)
- mitigates risk in the development program by getting team members to plan out the whole development process and obtaining management buy-in (which helps with project initiation and budget justification)
- ensures efficient utilization of project resources
- can create credibility with regulatory agencies
- can result in a timely approval for a product, meeting business objectives

- expedites patient access to new and improved products and therapies

The process of creating a regulatory strategy does not need to take months or a year to complete. Regulatory can provide the research, information and intelligence and come to the table with a reasonable working draft for team discussion (which might take a month or two), but once the initial draft is done, this process requires the team to sit down and focus on the task at hand, forgetting competing interests, to develop the first collective team draft of the strategy. Participating in strategy development also requires the team to act and agree, so all team members can stand behind the decisions made.

## FDA's or Other Regulatory Agency's Perspective

FDA, when conducting a review of a marketing application, reverse engineers the application, looking at all the facets of the strategy described to see whether the necessary components of a successful drug development program are addressed, incorporating the regulations, guidance documents and past precedents. If the company's team does not take the time to put together a strategy, FDA will figure this out quickly (which could result in a Refuse to File or Complete Response letter).

Planning for success can occur when the team sits down and discusses drug development issues that will need to be addressed at all stages of drug development. It is better, and ultimately less expensive, to prospectively expect and mitigate these issues than react to them as they arise or when the agency brings them to the company's attention.

## Who manages and updates the strategy?

The project management department incorporates goals into the timeline. Goals and achievements are tracked on a monthly basis, specifically progress toward reaching milestones (or not). Tracking and updating usually are done by project management in a core team meeting.

## How to Deal With Changes in Strategy

Even if 40 or 100 hours are spent creating the initial strategy, it will change over time. Documenting strategy is important so it can be modified over time. The team should be open to incorporating changes since the only constant is change. Changes will come from:
- new information about the drug itself
  o unexpected nonclinical or clinical safety signals
  o stability or dosing issues
- changes in the regulatory landscape
- new reviewers at the agency
- emerging safety information about the drug class or competitors' drugs

Some changes can be anticipated, and some are unexpected. The strategy should be updated as things change, and it should be viewed as a process that grows and changes with the drug.

## How do you know a strategy is successful?

There are various markers to indicate success including:
- product is approved in the US
- product is approved ex-US
- product is approved in multiple countries
- product has expanded indications approved

## Tools to Help With Strategy

A variety of tools can help the team develop a strategy or competitive analysis. Some are free, and some are for a fee. The for-fee tools provide summarized documentation and greatly aid in quickly composing a strategy. Following are specific strategy areas and the tools that can be used to help create the document.

### How to Find Drugs for a Disease, Indication or Therapeutic Area

When first starting on a new indication and laying out a competitive landscape and past precedents, it can be a challenge to find all the drugs used to treat that indication, whether it be approved or off label. A good place to start is a simple one, Drugs.com. When a search term such as "diabetes" is entered, this free website will pull up a list of all the drugs used to treat the indication and the different names of the same drug by country. The online Physician's Desk Reference (PDR) is another resource, but requires a subscription. Another for-fee tool to help locate all the drugs used to treat an indication, including the labels, is PharmaPendium.

### How to Learn Whether a Drug is Approved Someplace

To help put together a global strategy, finding out whether a precedent product has been approved can help the company develop its current product. Where can global drug approval databases be found? **Table 12-2** is a list of publically available sites that can be searched to find out whether a drug is marketed in a particular country. If these sites are not helpful, a public company's Securities and Exchange Commission filings might contain the information.

### History of the Indication

The RI professional needs to find and summarize the following information:
- What is the disease?
- How is the disease currently diagnosed (in the US and ex-US)?
- What is the course of the disease?
- How is the disease currently managed (in the US and ex-US)?
- What is the "gold standard" or standard of care, including all class of drugs to treat the disease (in the US and Ex-US)?

  o   Which is first line?
  o   Which is second line, etc.?

**Free Tools**
- WebMD (www.webmd.com)
- Drugs.com
- advocacy groups (such as www.diabetes.org)
- journal articles, especially meta-analysis articles (the majority, but not all, require subscriptions or are pay per article) via The National Library of Medicine's Medline (www.ncbi.nlm.nih.gov/pubmed)
- physicians working for the company or as key opinion leaders
- Google

**For-Fee Tools**
- PDR
- Martindale: The Complete Drug Reference
- Thomson Micromedex
- PharmaPendium
- NDA Pipeline
- indication profile from BioMed Tracker
- market analysis/research reports, such as www.reportlinker.com

### Therapeutic Area

When the RI professional is searching for competitor or therapeutic information about:
- clinical endpoints
- status of competitive drug(s)
- Advisory Committee Meeting findings
- withdrawals, rejections or safety alerts (black box warnings)

Both free and for-fee tools are available.

**Free Tools**
- NIH Clinicaltrials.gov
- WHO (International Clinical Trials Registry Portal)
- current controlled trials (controlled-trials.com)
- IFPMA Clinical Trial Portal
- JAPIC Clinical Trials Information

**Table 12-2. Sources to Check for Drug Approval**

| | |
|---|---|
| Australia—Register of Therapeutic Goods | www.ebs.tga.gov.au/ebs/ANZTPAR/PublicWeb.nsf/cuMedicines?OpenView |
| Hong Kong—Registered Pharmaceuticals | www.psdh.gov.hk/eps/productSearchSimpleAction.do |
| India—Drugs approved for marketing | www.cdsco.nic.in/listofdrugapprovedmain.html |
| Japanese Pharmaceutical Reference | www.e-search.ne.jp/~jpr/jpr_db/eindex.html |
| Malaysia—Products approved at DCA Meetings | http://portal.bpfk.gov.my/index.cfm?menuid=40 |
| New Zealand—Consumer Medicine Info | www.medsafe.govt.nz/Consumers/cmi/CMIForm.asp |
| Canada Drug Product Database Search | www.hc-sc.gc.ca/dhp-mps/prodpharma/databasdon/index_e.html/ |
| EudraPharm (Product information for centrally authorized products) | eudrapharm.eu/eudrapharm/welcome.do |
| EU MRI index (Product information and Public Assessment Reports for products authorized via Mutual Recognition Procedure and Decentralized Procedure) | www.hma.eu/mri.html |
| EU Register of designated orphan products | ec.europa.eu/health/documents/community-register/html/orphreg.htm#o012 |
| Belgium—Federal Public Service Health (List of authorized products and list of marketing authorizations withdrawals) | www.fagg-afmps.be/en/items-HOME/databases/index.jsp |
| Czech Republic—State Institute for Drug Control—Product information | www.sukl.cz/modules/medication/search.php |
| France—National Agency of Medicine and Health Product Safety (ANSM)—Product information and Public Assessment Reports | ansm.sante.fr/Mediatheque/Publications/Rapports-Syntheses-Rapports-publics-d-evaluation#med http://ansm.sante.fr/Services/Repertoire-des-medicaments |
| Irish Medicine's Board Public Assessment Reports | www.imb.ie/EN/Human-Medicines/New-EU-Pharmacovigilance-Legislation/Search-for-Medicines-Information/Public-Assessment-Reports-.aspx |
| Netherlands—Medicines Information Data Bank | www.cbg-meb.nl/CBG/en/human-medicines/geneesmiddeleninformatiebank/default.htm |
| UK—Medicines and Healthcare products Regulatory Agency Public Assessment Reports | www.mhra.gov.uk/Safetyinformation/Medicinesinformation/PARs/index.htm |
| US FDA CDER approved NDAs (Drugs@FDA) | www.accessdata.fda.gov/scripts/cder/drugsatfda/ |
| US FDA CBER approved biologics | www.fda.gov/BiologicsBloodVaccines/ucm121134.htm |

- Centerwatch.com

**For-Fee Tools**
- Trialtrove (www.citeline.com/products/trialtrove/)
- PharmaPendium (www.pharmapendium.com)

### Competitive Products

Why should a company look at its competitors' products?

- to help understand its product's place in the market
- to understand the indication and treatment options
- to use parts of a competitor's regulatory strategy to aid the company's pathway and avoid pitfalls
- for unapproved products, the company needs to know the competitor's product type and the stage of their clinical trials (press releases, review articles, company

websites, market research reports, clinical trial registries)
- to help build development strategies by looking at:
  o regulatory history of competitor's approved products
  o product's regulatory history and why it has not been approved or developed further
  o competitor's labeling
  o registration procedures and approval trends

**Free Tools**
- Drugs@FDA (www.accessdata.fda.gov/scripts/cder/drugsatfda/index.cfm)
- Clinicaltrials.gov
- Drugs.com or www.drugs.com/new-drug-applications.html
- www.hoovers.com
- www.fiercebiotech.com (indication-specific press releases)
- Regulatorium.com (worldwide links for global approvals)
- Google searches
- company press releases and websites

**For-Fee Tools**
- IND/NDA pipeline information databases
  o Inteleos
  o Thomson Reuters Partnering (formerly IDdb3)
  o Citeline's Pipeline (formerly Pharmaprojects)
  o Sagient Research BioMed Tracker
  o Springer HealthCare AdisInsight
  o www.medtrack.com
- PharmaPendium (approved drugs and labels)

## Competitive Label Analysis

Reviewing competitive labels of approved products to understand label claims will drive a company's clinical study primary and secondary objectives, endpoints and

adverse event profile. This is a very manual process; no tools yet exist to complete such an analysis quickly. The following sites can be used for labeling searches:
- DailyMed (download electronic files) dailymed.nlm.nih.gov/dailymed/about.cfm
- Drugs@FDA
- FDA: labels.fda.gov
- Drugs.com

For a competitive label analysis, once the company has a list of all the approved drugs to treat the indication, the RI professional should:
- get a copy of all the labels from FDA.gov or PharmaPendium (if it has a subscription)
- review all labels
- briefly summarize the highlights for each drug, by section or drug class by section

## Past Precedent Review

Part of any regulatory strategy is reviewing what has been submitted previously to health authorities. If a competitor has already received approval in a specific drug class or indication, reading its approval filing can help the company gain insight on what the agency found acceptable for a clinical development program and study endpoints. For abbreviated submissions, it is imperative to know what has been done and what innovator safety and clinical data can be relied upon for the filing (please see Chapter 6 Drug Approval Summaries and Past Precedents for more detailed information on how to collect and summarize this information).

The goal of researching precedents includes:
- the history of the molecule, is it:
  o first in class (this is a more difficult path since the drug is a true "pioneer" and requires more FDA negotiation)
  o seventh "me-too" drug on the market
  o somewhere in between

- whether the drug or drug class has been approved before
- precedents need to be within the past 15 years; applications reviewed and/or approved prior to 1997 are not pertinent since ICH implementation has changed the registration requirements and data required for a marketing application—if reviewing a drug approved prior to 1997:
  o The application would be found deficient by today's standards.
  o Additional testing or tests will be required to bring the filing and data up to current standards.
- more than one application can be relied upon for precedent information

What is the goal of the review?
- When was the drug approved?
- What was the reviewing division?
- How many patients in the safety database were required for approval or postapproval?

- How many clinical trials were conducted?
  o What were the clinical end-points used for each trial?
  o What were the initial clinical objectives (label claims) and how did these change over the development process?
  o What were the issues with the trials (NDA review issues)?
- Did the company apply for any waivers and did FDA grant them?
- What nonclinical trials were required versus those conducted?
- What were the final label claims?

**Free Tools**
- Drugs@FDA
- Global EPARs, et al: www.regu-latorium.com/intelligence-links.html

**Fee Tools**
- PharmaPendium (use a key word search to pull up applicable documents to review)
- consultants

# CHAPTER 13

# Guidance Document Summaries

## What is a guidance document?

Guidance documents represent the agency's current thinking on a particular subject and establish policies intended to achieve internal agency consistency for inspection and enforcement procedures. These documents provide guidelines on the processing, content, evaluation and approval of applications, and the design, production, manufacturing and testing of regulated products.

In the US, guidance documents are not regulations or laws; they are not enforceable, through either administrative actions or the courts. An alternative approach may be used if such approach satisfies the requirements of the applicable statute, regulations or both. However, if an alternative approach is used, it must be reviewed by the agency to ensure it is acceptable. In other countries, guidance documents are laws and enforceable, so the company must understand the guidance document policy of the country in which it is working.

## Why summarize it?

Time is limited during the workday, and the amount of reading can be overwhelming. However, when a new guidance document is issued, it is the RI professional's job to ensure the executive staff and all the regulatory and other team members affected by the guidance document are kept informed.

Creating a guidance document summary is part of landscape management since it is impossible to understand the landscape without knowing all the requirements. A guidance document summary, distributed within a few days of the guidance document's issuance, creates actionable intelligence that an executive can use to understand how it may affect the company or its products, what needs to be implemented, the timeframe for implementation and what resources are needed to implement the change.

## What to Summarize

What to include in a summary varies depending on the type of guidance document since their topics, formats and information can be very different, so the following should be used only as a guideline:

- title
- date issued
- draft or final

**Table 13-1. Sample Guidance Document Template**

| GUIDANCE DOCUMENT SUMMARY | |
|---|---|
| **Title:**<br>**Date of Guidance/Summary:**<br>**Draft/Final?** | **Category:** |
| **Statute/Regulations Referenced or Affected** | |
| **SUMMARY** | |
| | |
| | |
| | |
| *Changes from Draft Guidance* | |
| | |
| | |
| *Implementation/Impact Recommendations* | |
| | |
| *Timeline for Implementation* | |
| | |
| *Comments on Draft to be Submitted* | |
| | |
| | |
| Definitions Used:<br>1 | |
| 2 | |
| 3 | |
| | |
| IND Section Affected: | |
| NDA Section Affected: | |

- if comments are requested, will the organization submit them or not (include the due date); if so, the RI professional should draft recommended comments for review
- guidance category (it is easier to organize in a database if categories are assigned consistently)
- regulations or laws affected
- summary of the guidance document
- summary of any changes since the last edition of the document
- implementation or impact recommendations (to company development programs or practices)
- timeline or deadline for implementation (if applicable); this is especially important if the deadline is prior to the date the updated regulation will be codified
- any new definitions introduced or key to interpreting the document
- references to any other documents that are key to understanding the guidance
- any filings that might be affected by the new guidance to help upper management plan for implementation and submission planning
- a template for a new type of submission if provided by the regulatory agency (such as a Pediatric Investigational Plan provided by EMA) or a plan for template creation (such as for the Pediatric Study Plan guidance issued by FDA)

## Draft vs. Final

When a draft guidance document is issued, it typically is open for comment for 60 days or per the usual timeframe for a certain country (some countries do not allow commenting; they just issue the final draft). Once comments are received, they are considered and either implemented or not. It is always interesting to see what has changed between the draft and final documents. But, it is important to capture what the final document says because if the summary is based just on the draft (assuming the final version has been issued), not on the final, it could lead people astray in their interpretation and implementation of the final guidance.

## Where to Find Guidance Documents—US

- drugs and biologics www.fda.gov/Drugs/GuidanceComplianceRegulatoryInformation/default.htm
- devices www.fda.gov/MedicalDevices/DeviceRegulationandGuidance/GuidanceDocuments/default.htm

## Where to Find Scientific Guidelines—EU

- drugs and biologics www.ema.europa.eu/ema/index.jsp?curl=pages/regulation/landing/human_medicines_regulatory.jsp&mid=WC0b01ac058001ff89
- devices ec.europa.eu/health/medical-devices/documents/guidelines/index_en.htm

## Guidance Documents—Ex-US

Please see: www.regulatorium.com/intelligence-links.html.

**Table 13-2. Guidance Document Summary Example**

| GUIDANCE DOCUMENT SUMMARY | |
|---|---|
| **Title**: Diabetes Mellitus—Evaluating Cardiovascular Risk in New Antidiabetic Therapies to Treat Type 2 Diabetes | **Category**: Development of drugs and therapeutic biologics |
| | **Date of Guidance/Summary**:  December 2008 |

**Statute/Regulations Referenced or Affected**
- ICH E8 General Considerations for Clinical Trials
- ICH E9 Statistical Principals for Clinical Trials

**SUMMARY**

- Specifically, this guidance recommends how to demonstrate that a new antidiabetic therapy to treat type-2 diabetes is not associated with an unacceptable increase in cardiovascular risk.
- Tight glucose control in patients with type 1 diabetes reduces the development and progression of chronic diabetic complications (retinopathy, nephropathy and neuropathy).
- Long-term glycemic control in patients with type 2 diabetes results in reduced risks of micro-vascular complications. This is based on changes in HbA1c, and this end-point reflects a beneficial effect in immediate clinical consequences of diabetes.

*Implementation/Impact Advice*

Sponsors should demonstrate that a new therapy will not result in an unacceptable increase in cardiovascular risks by planning to conduct cardiovascular studies during their development program.

*Clinical Studies in Planning Stage:*
- Independent cardiovascular endpoints, such as cardiovascular mortality, myocardial infarction and stroke, hospitalization for acute coronary syndrome, urgent re-vascularization procedures should be established in all Phase 2 and 3 trials.
- All Phase 2 and 3 trials should be appropriately designed to enable meta-analysis at the time of completion. Hence, patients at higher risk of cardiovascular events, such as patients with advanced disease, elderly patients and patients with some renal impairment should be included.
- Sponsors should provide a protocol describing statistical methods for meta-analysis, and these studies should typically last three to six months to obtain enough events and data on long term cardiovascular risk.
- Studies should be spread across Phase 2 and Phase 3 trials and should explore similarities or differences in subgroups (age, sex, race) if possible.

*For Completed Studies*
- Sponsors should compare the incidence of important cardiovascular events occurring with investigational drug to the incidence of same types of events occurring with the control group to show that upper bound of two-sided 95% confidence interval for the estimated risk ratio is less than 1.8.
- This could be accomplished based on meta-analysis of Phase 2 and 3 trials, or an additional single large safety trial should be conducted.
- If the upper bound of two-sided 95% confidence interval for estimated risk is between 1.3 and 1.8, a postmarketing trial will be necessary to definitively show that the risk ratio is less than 1.3.
- If the upper bound of two-sided 95% confidence interval for estimated risk is less than 1.3 and the overall risk-benefit analysis supports approval, a postmarketing trial may not be necessary.
- The final report should contain sufficient details such as graphic plots by study, subgroups and overall risk ratio and a data set that would allow a verification of the findings.

Definitions Used:
1. *Diabetes mellitus:* Diabetes mellitus is a chronic metabolic disorder characterized by hyperglycemia caused by defective insulin secretion, resistance to insulin action or a combination of both. Alterations of lipid and protein metabolism also are important manifestations of these defects in insulin secretion or action.
2. *Type 1 diabetes:* Type 1 diabetes is a form of diabetes mellitus that is immune-related or idiopathic.
3. *Type 2 diabetes:* Type 2 diabetes is a form of diabetes mellitus with a complex pathophysiology that combines progressive insulin resistance and beta cell failure.

CHAPTER 14

# Citizen's Petition

## What is a petition?

Per 21 CFR 10.3, a petition means a petition, application or other document requesting the commissioner to establish, amend or revoke a regulation or order, or to take or not to take any other form of administrative action, under the laws administered by FDA.

## What is a Citizen's Petition?

Citizen's Petitions are another way to influence FDA through submitting a petition to the agency to issue, change or cancel a regulation, or to take other action.

## Why would a Citizen's Petition be filed?

A company would file a Citizen's Petition to:
- block entry of a generic product or, conversely, to allow a generic product to market
- request a new ingredient be allowed in an OTC product
- allow a new product to market
- remove a product from the market
- request a change in labeling
- request tighter regulations

## Who can file a Citizen's Petition?

Individuals sometimes submit petitions, but most come from regulated industry, lawyers or consumer groups.

## What must a petition contain?

FDA spends considerable time and staff resources processing petitions, so the request must be valid and not waste the agency's time and resources. A petition must contain enough information for FDA to properly evaluate and make a decision on the request. A petition must contain the following sections (additional details to follow):

### What is the requested action?

What rule, order or other administrative action does the petitioner want FDA to issue, amend or revoke?

### Statement of Grounds

A full statement, in a well-organized format, of the factual and legal grounds on which the petitioner relies, including all relevant information and views on which the petitioner relies, as well as representative information known to the petitioner that is unfavorable to the petitioner's position.

### Environmental impact

This generally is required if the petition requests approval of food or color additives, drugs, biological products, animal drugs or certain medical devices, or of a food to be categorized as GRAS (generally recognized as safe).

### Official certification statement

"The undersigned certifies, that, to the best knowledge and belief of the undersigned, this petition includes all information and views on which the petition relies, and that it includes representative data and information known to the petition which are unfavorable to the petition."

> (Signature)
> (Name of petitioner)
> (Mailing address)
> (Telephone number)

### Identifying Information

The petition must be signed and include the petitioner's address and phone number.

In addition, some petitions may require information on the petition's economic impact. This information is required only if FDA requests it after review of the petition.

## What is an interested person?

An interested person or any person who will be adversely affected means a person who submits a petition or comment or objection or otherwise asks to participate in an informal or formal administrative proceeding or court action. The person who submits the citizen's petition does not have to be a US citizen.

## Action Requested

Depending on the petition's focus, this section must contain the following information:

- If the petition requests the commissioner to issue, amend or revoke a regulation, the exact wording of the existing regulation (if any) and the proposed regulation or amendment requested.
- If the petition requests the commissioner to issue, amend or revoke an order, a copy of the exact wording of the citation to the existing order (if any) and the exact wording requested for the proposed order.
- If the petition requests the commissioner to take or refrain from taking any other form of administrative action, the specific action or relief requested.

## Environmental Impact

The application must have a claim for categorical exclusion under 21 CFR 25.30, 25.31, 25.32, 25.33, or 25.34 or an environmental assessment under 25.40.

## Economic Impact

The following information is to be submitted only when requested by the commissioner following review of the petition: A statement of the effect of requested action on:

1. cost (and price) increases to industry, government and consumers
2. productivity of wage earners, businesses or government
3. competition
4. supply of important materials, products or services
5. employment
6. energy supply or demand

## Where to Send the Petition

A Citizen's Petition should be sent to:
Division of Dockets Management
Food and Drug Administration
Department of Health and Human Services
5630 Fishers Lane, Rm. 1061
Rockville, MD 20852

FDA currently does not accept emailed petitions. Petitions must be mailed or delivered to: Division of Dockets Management, at the above address.

## Submitting Petitions

For more information on submitting petitions, and sample formats, consult 21 CFR Sections 10.30, 10.33, and 10.35.

## What happens at FDA when a Citizen's Petition is received?

The agency receives about 200 petitions yearly. Once a valid Citizen's Petition is received, it will be stamped with the date of filing and assigned a docket number. The docket number identifies the file established by the Division of Dockets Management for all submissions relating to the petition.

Related petitions may be filed together and given the same docket number. The Division of Dockets Management will notify the petitioner promptly, in writing, of the petition's filing and docket number.

The public will be made aware of the petition through publication in the *Federal Register* and on Regulations.gov, and the public will be allowed to comment on the petition.

Interested parties and the public can submit information relating to the petition to the public docket, and these submissions are accessible to the public via Regulations.gov. The information is added to the docket for that petition and made available to the public.

## Can a Citizen's Petition be amended?

A petitioner may supplement, amend or withdraw a petition in writing, without agency approval and without prejudice to resubmission at any time, until the commissioner rules on the petition, unless the petition has been referred for a hearing. After a ruling or referral, a petition may be supplemented, amended or withdrawn only with the commissioner's approval.

## How long does it take for an FDA review?

The commissioner shall furnish a response to each petitioner within 180 days of receipt of the petition.

## Review Tools

In reviewing a petition, the commissioner may use the following procedures:
1. conferences, meetings, discussions and correspondence
2. a hearing
3. a *Federal Register* notice requesting information and views
4. a proposal to issue, amend or revoke a regulation
5. any other specific public procedure

## FDA's Response to a Citizen's Petition

The information and materials that serve as the basis for FDA's decision on the Citizen's Petition are explained in the response to the petition. FDA's response to a petition usually involves an in-depth analysis of the issues raised in the petition and an extensive explanation of the agency's rationale for its determination. At the time the response is issued, FDA places in the public docket any published literature that is referenced in the response but has not been placed in the public docket by the petitioner or by commenters.

Additionally, FDA provides the public with a detailed rationale in the response to the Citizen's Petition and provides the public with access to the documents that serve as the basis for FDA's determination.

## Citizen's Petition Outcome

The response will either:
- approve the petition, in which case the commissioner shall concurrently take appropriate action (e.g., publication of a *Federal Register* notice) implementing the approval
- deny the petition
- provide a tentative response, indicating why the agency has been

unable to reach a decision on the petition, e.g., because of the existence of other agency priorities, or a need for additional information; the tentative response also may indicate the likely ultimate agency response, and may specify when a final response may be furnished

## Timeline for a Citizen's Petition Decision/Outcome

Ultimately, FDA management decides whether to grant a petition. But first, agency staff evaluate it, a process that may take several weeks to more than a year, depending on the issue's complexity. After FDA grants or denies the petition, the agency will notify the petitioner directly. If not satisfied, the petitioner may take the matter to court.

**References**
*Guidance for Industry: Citizen Petitions and Petitions for Stay of Action Subject to Section 505(q) of the Federal Food, Drug, and Cosmetic Act*, June 2011

Linda Bowen, Slides for Regulatory Intelligence - Commenting, Regulatory Intelligence Course, Temple University, 2011

# White Papers

## What is a white paper?

A white paper is a government report or authoritative "position paper" that provides in-depth analysis meant to inform the reader about the topic of choice, like a hybrid of a brochure, magazine article, a review or meta-analysis journal article but without the formal publication or peer review process. White papers also are used extensively in marketing and sales literature intended to be persuasive, and have a use in RI.

## How do you use white papers in RI?

White papers have a variety of RI uses, including helping readers understand an issue, solve a problem, make a decision, explain or justify a position or just to inform. Specifically, in RI, white papers are used to:

- provide a summary of a particular topic, such as a summary and analysis of all orphan drug regulations around the world
- support a particular position (for a trade organization, internally to support certain procedures or to send to FDA to support a point or a position outside of a formal submission or in response to a meeting question or information request), justify not adhering to a guidance document or for selecting clinical endpoints in an orphan clinical trial that have never been used before
- illustrate best practices when holding a meeting with a regulator
- outline all the drugs currently used to treat a particular indication (approved and investigational)
- summarize new legislation, such as *PDUFA*
- interpret a guidance document based on a company's SOPs

Unless used for marketing, white papers typically are kept company confidential and for internal use only (unless being submitted to a regulatory agency, in which case they are sent only to that agency).

## Typical White Paper Format

Typically, a white paper uses the following format, but this can be modified to fit the message the white paper is trying to deliver or support. A white paper usually contains graphics and tables to communicate a vast amount of information in four pages or less:

- Executive Summary (this does not have to be included, but it can provide an abstract or high-level summary of the entire document for those who want to get to the point of the paper in 400 words or less)
- Objective (this can be clearly stated or woven into an introductory paragraph)
- Background (to quickly acquaint the reader with the topic)
- Problem Statement or Issue (this, too, can be woven into an introductory paragraph)
- Proposed Resolution or Solution (with support from the literature)
- Conclusion (discussion of the information presented and a restatement of the solution)
- References (if needed)

This is similar to the regulatory research format, but instead of being segmented in a table format, it is cohesive text telling a story with graphic images.

## Gear Toward the Specific Audience

A white paper always should be geared to the reader's education level—if it is highly scientific, the reader needs to understand the more technical jargon being used. If the intent is to communicate a general summary of a topic (such as how to initiate a clinical trial in 90+ countries and the documentation needed) to a whole development team, the focus should be on keeping the terminology and concepts accessible and simple.

## Length

The optimum length for a white paper is four pages, typically the length of time a person will devote to reading a position paper. However, it can be as long 20 or more pages and as short as one page.

## FDA White Papers

FDA uses white papers prior to issuing a pre-guidance document to build support for a position or to receive feedback prior to publishing the document in the *Federal Register* for formal comments. It also issues them to aid the public in understanding its perspective on specific topics.

### FDA White Paper Examples

- meta-analysis www.fda.gov/downloads/Drugs/NewsEvents/UCM372069.pdf
- radiation exposure www.fda.gov/Radiation-EmittingProducts/RadiationSafety/RadiationDoseReduction/ucm199994.htm
- dental amalgam www.fda.gov/medicaldevices/productsandmedicalprocedures/dentalproducts/dentalamalgam/ucm171117.htm
- *PDUFA* summary www.fda.gov/forindustry/userfees/prescriptiondruguserfee/ucm119253.htm
- clinical www.fda.gov/downloads/drugs/scienceresearch/researchareas/ucm091457.pdf

### Other White Paper Examples

- rare diseases www.everylifefoundation.org/wp-content/uploads/2013/06/White-Paper-V12-CLEAN.pdf
- medical services www.ama-assn.org/resources/doc/psa/standardization-prior-auth-white-paper.pdf
- 510(k) process www.elsevierbi.com/~/media/205258BC16894600AB9913836E9B72C3 and http://advamed.org/res/317/modifications-to-be-cleared-in-commercial-distribution
- conference overview journal.pda.org/content/68/1/2

CHAPTER 16

# Regulatory Policy

## What is regulatory policy?

A policy is a statement of intent and is implemented as a principle or protocol to guide decisions and achieve rational outcomes. Policy differs from rules or law; while law can compel or prohibit behaviors, policy merely guides actions toward those that are most likely to achieve a desired outcome such as to change or implement a law and in turn a regulation.

## Regulatory Policy as an RI Function

Regulatory policies are created by each company to align with company goals across multiple regions. These regulatory policies are then implemented by the RI professional exerting influence on the legislative process and health authorities through a variety of methodologies. This position can be part of RI, legal or government affairs. In addition, this type of RI professional is proactive in influencing policy and shaping the landscape whereas RI operations monitors the landscape looking for changes and reacting to them.

### *Typical RI Policy Responsibilities*

Typical responsibilities include:

- lobbying or influencing the outcome of draft laws and regulatory guidelines
- high level surveillance: tracking key developments from health authorities, trade associations, professional associations, working groups and special interest groups and any other organization or group external to the company that can affect the company's regulatory outcomes
- in-depth impact analyses of upcoming laws
- drafting responses to public consultations or providing comments on pending regulation
  - o   contributing to favorable regulatory landscape
  - o   assuring strategic interests are reflected in guidances and regulations
- maintaining active memberships in associations
- tracking issues

Other responsibilities include:
- speaking with one voice to health authorities and trade associations on regulatory policies

- industry colleagues—networking with other locally based RI policy professionals to help achieve a common goal
- providing feedback to corporate customers on regulatory landscape
- networking with health authority management and opinion leaders
- managing external expert relationships

Typically, these individuals have offices near the relevant legislative and regulatory bodies, e.g., Washington, DC in the US. These individuals usually are former regulatory authority reviewers with experience with agency processes and knowledge of how to influence the legislative process.

## What is regulatory policy usually called?

A variety of titles are used for those RI professionals who work to shape policy:
- FDA liaison
- regulatory policy
- regulatory strategist
- regulatory relations
- scientific and regulatory intelligence

## Health Authority Interaction

Typically, RI policy professionals are the face the company presents to the health authority and usually are ex-employees of that agency. By interacting with health authority personnel, the RI policy professional is able to understand, from an insider's perspective, the issues important to the agency, the types of issues with which it is dealing, upcoming legislation and the health authority's reaction to it and how it plans to implement that legislation. Additionally, they also:
- help guide and set policy with FDA (or other health authorities) by influencing the policies made
- predict future legislation or policies based on trends

- establish or build rapport with agency staff
- identify where industry and the health authority can benefit from collaborations
- meet FDA (or other health authority) management and opinion leaders
- offer to provide the health authority with the "industry side"

## Trade Association Participation

RI policy professionals are members of, interact with and participate in trade association meetings. Participation in a trade association by an RI policy professional includes:
- establishing or building rapport with trade associations such as PhRMA, BIO, IFPMA
- serving as point of contact for their companies on regulatory issues
  o ensuring company receives timely information on changes in the regulatory landscape and their potential impact
  o providing timely and thoughtful responses to trade association inquires and expecting the same in return
  o providing comments on pending legislation, regulations or guidance that are in line with company goals to be incorporated into the trade association's response
- participating in, recruiting for and leading work groups or committees to prepare position papers

## Lobbying

Dictionary.com defines Lobbying as,
- "a group of persons who work or conduct a campaign to influence members of a legislature to vote according to the group's special interest"

- "to solicit or try to influence the votes of members of a legislative body", to try to influence the actions of (public officials, especially legislators)"
- "to urge or procure the passage of (a bill), by lobbying."

Therefore, "Lobbying" is when an individual asks policymakers to take a specific position on a specific piece of legislation, and a lobbyist is a person who tries to influence legislation on behalf of a special interest or a member of a lobby. Lobby groups and their members sometimes also write legislation and encourage support for bills among legislators.

RI policy interacts with lobbyists in a variety of models including:

- supporting lobbying efforts and advising staff on health authority matters
- lobbying directly on regulatory issues to the health authority and legislators
- keeping lobbying and regulatory/ scientific issues distinct (Minimal to no contact with the health authority and legislators, working directly with lobbyists, special interest and advocacy groups.)

## Working Groups

A working group is an *ad hoc* group of volunteer, industry, subject-matter experts working together to achieve specific goals as defined by the group. The term "working groups" also refers to task groups, steering groups, workgroups, or technical advisory groups. The lifespan of a working group can be from a few months to several years. The rules for who can participate in a working group and how a working group makes decisions vary considerably among organizations. These groups meet and make decisions on specific topics; output from a working group can include:

- an informational document
- a standard
- resolution of problems related to a system or network

- continuous improvement
- research
- guidance document

These working groups can be formed by a trade association to deal with specific topics or be standalone organizations.

RI policy professionals volunteer to sit on working group committees (not health authority committees unless invited to do so) to influence the outcome of standards, research, proposals, legislation, white papers, guidance documents or policies issued.

### Working Group Examples

RI policy professionals lead and participate in working groups such as:

- ISO working groups
- International Conference on Harmonisation
- Bioethics Council
- Non Biological Complex Drugs Working Group (NBCD) - www.tipharma.com/ pharmaceutical-research-projects/drug-discovery-development-and-utilisation/ nonbiologicalcomplexdrug-sworkinggroupnbcd.html
- Working Group on Pharmaceutical Safety www.4rxsafety.org/

### Trade Organizations with Working Group Examples

- International Pharmaceutical Federation (FIP) working groups fip.org/?page=pp_info_activities
- Pharmaceutical Research and Manufacturers of America Working Groups www.phrma. org/
- BIO bio.org

### Health Authority Working Group Examples

- Pharmaceutical Working Groups—Pharmaceutical cGMPs for the 21st Century: A Risk-Based Approach: www.fda.gov/Drugs/

DevelopmentApprovalProcess/
Manufacturing/QuestionsandAn-
swersonCurrentGoodManufac-
turingPracticescGMPforDrugs/
ucm071991.htm
- Pharmaceutical Quality Standards
Working Group—Charter: www.
fda.gov/AboutFDA/CentersOf-
fices/OfficeofMedicalProduct-
sandTobacco/CDER/ucm088791.
htm#
- EU Pharmaceutical Forum—
ec.europa.eu/enterprise/
sectors/healthcare/competi-
tiveness/pharmaceutical-forum/
index_en.htm
- Australian Pharmaceutical
Industry Working Group—www.
innovation.gov.au/INDUSTRY/
PHARMACEUTICALSAND-
HEALTHTECHNOLOGIES/
PHARMACEUTICALS/Pages/
PharmaceuticalIndustryWorking-
Group.aspx

## Advocacy Groups

Advocacy groups use various forms of
advocacy to influence public opinion and/
or policy. They vary considerably in size,
influence and motive, and use varied
methods to try to achieve their aims

including lobbying, media campaigns,
publicity stunts, polls, research and policy
briefings. RI works with advocacy groups
that represent patients with specific diseases to help learn about the disease, the
patients who have the disease, caregiver
issues, physicians who treat the disease,
current treatments and unmet medical
needs, and to publicize and help drive
enrollment in clinical trials. This is especially important for orphan indications.

## Special Interest Groups

A Special Interest Group (SIG) is a community that comes together to advance a
specific area of knowledge, learning or technology where members cooperate to effect
or to produce solutions within their particular field, and may communicate, meet
and organize conferences. They may at
times also advocate or lobby on a particular
issue or on a range of issues, but generally are distinct from advocacy groups that
normally are organized for specific political
aims. The distinction is not clear cut, however, and some organizations can adapt and
change their focus over time. If it would
benefit a particular company, the RI professional can establish a relationship with the
SIG, lobby through it or in conjunction with
it, or work with it on a particular topic.

# CHAPTER 17

# Tracking Legislation, Regulations and Guidance Documents

How legislation, bills, laws, regulations, directives and guidance documents, etc., come into effect varies by country. The RI professional needs to know a country's particular process to be able to work and survey the landscape effectively within that country. Because describing the global legislation process is beyond the scope of this book, the US process is described in this chapter as a model for the information of which an RI analyst needs to be aware.

## Legislature

The US Congress is the legislative body of the federal government. It is bicameral, consisting of two houses, the Senate and the House of Representatives. Legislators in both are members of Congress, though usually only a representative is called a congressman, congresswoman or congressperson. Both senators and representatives are chosen through direct election by US citizens.

Congress derives all its legislative powers from the US Constitution. The House and Senate are generally equal partners in the legislative process (legislation cannot be enacted without the consent of both chambers). However, the Constitution grants each chamber unique powers unavailable to the other, as well. This provides a balance of power between the two legislative chambers.

Legislation can be introduced in either house of Congress by any member and can be sent to Congress for consideration by the US president. Proposed legislation usually is sent to the appropriate congressional committee to review, revise and recommend action.

## Bill

Most legislative proposals are in the form of bills and are designated as H.R. (House of Representatives) or S. (Senate), depending on the house in which they originate, and are numbered consecutively in the order in which they are introduced during each Congress.

Public bills deal with general issues and become public laws or acts, if approved by Congress and signed by the president.

Private bills deal with individual matters such as claims against the federal government, immigration and naturalization cases, land titles, etc., and become private laws if approved and signed.

## Act

An act is legislation that has passed both houses of Congress and been approved by the president, or passed over his veto, thus becoming law. This term also is used technically for a bill that has been passed by one house of Congress.

## Law

Laws may be initiated in either chamber of Congress, the House of Representatives or the Senate.

A law is a bill or joint resolution (other than amendments to the Constitution) passed by both houses of Congress and approved by the president. Bills and joint resolutions vetoed by the president, but overridden by Congress, also become public law.

## Law Interpreted by FDA

After congressional bills become laws, federal departments and agencies are responsible for enforcing those laws through regulations. Departments and agencies develop regulations through the federal rulemaking process, most commonly through a notice-and-comment process. In general, departments and agencies publish proposed rules that are open for public comment; after a specified period of time, the department or agency publishes a final rule based on public comments and other information.

## What is a regulation (US)?

A regulation is an agency rule of general or particular applicability and future effect issued under a law administered by the commissioner or relating to administrative practices and procedures. Each agency regulation will be published in the *Federal Register* and codified in the Code of Federal Regulations.

An agency cannot issue a rule unless granted authority to do so by law.

Rule and regulation are synonymous terms and are used interchangeably.

## What is the *Federal Register*?

The *Federal Register* is a legal newspaper published every business day by the National Archives and Records Administration; it is the official newspaper of the US Government. It provides legal notice of administrative rules and notices and presidential documents in a comprehensive, uniform manner. The *Federal Register* contains:

- federal agency regulations
- proposed rules and public notices
- executive orders
- proclamations
- other presidential documents
- meeting notices
- draft and final guidance documents

The *Federal Register* can be accessed at www.archives.gov/federal-register/the-federal-register/.

## Code of Federal Regulations (CFR)

The Code of Federal Regulations (CFR) is the codification of the general and permanent rules published in the *Federal Register* by federal government executive departments and agencies. It is divided into 50 titles that represent broad areas subject to federal regulation. Each CFR volume is updated once each calendar year and is issued on a quarterly basis.

- Titles 1-16 are updated as of 1 January
- Titles 17-27 are updated as of 1 April
- Titles 28-41 are updated as of 1 July
- Titles 42-50 are updated as of 1 October

Each title is divided into chapters, which usually bear the name of the issuing agency. Each chapter is further subdivided into parts that cover specific regulatory areas. Large parts may be subdivided into subparts. All parts are organized in sections, and most citations in the CFR are provided at the section level. The CFR can be accessed at www.

gpo.gov/fdsys/browse/collectionCfr.
action?collectionCode=CFR.

Drugs, devices and biologics are regulated under CFR Title 21.

## Making Regulations

One of the most common ways agencies create regulations is through "informal rulemaking." In this type of rulemaking, agencies usually will publish a proposed rule in the *Federal Register* that contains both a "codified" part of the regulation (the actual rules that, when finalized, will appear in the CFR) and a "preamble," which is a discussion of why and how the agency thinks the rules will accomplish the mission. In addition, there will be a cost-benefit analysis (Preliminary Regulatory Impact Analysis) of the rules, which is required by executive order (from the president), and an Initial Regulatory Flexibility Analysis (IRFA), which is an analysis of how the regulation will affect small businesses or other small entities.

Before putting out the proposed rule or proposal, the agency may publish an advanced notice of proposed rulemaking (ANPR) in the *Federal Register*, or it may meet with various constituencies to solicit comments on how the rule should be crafted or issue a white paper to provide its position on an issue. Once a proposed rule has been published in the *Federal Register*, anyone may send the agency a written comment on the proposal. A time limit for submitting comments is specified in the proposal.

The final rule also is published in the *Federal Register*, where the agency sets the date by which the regulated community must comply with the rule. In the final rule, unless the agency certifies it will not have a significant economic impact on a substantial number of small entities, the agency will publish a Final Regulatory Flexibility Analysis addressing the small business impact and small business comments that were raised during the comment period for the proposed rule.

## Proposed Rules

When FDA plans to issue a new regulation or revise an existing one, it places an announcement in the *Federal Register* on the day the public comment period begins.

In the *Federal Register*, the "notice of proposed rulemaking" describes the planned regulation and provides background on the issue.

## Docket

FDA's Dockets Management Office is the official repository for the administrative proceedings and rulemaking documents for FDA.

Dockets Management is administered by the Federal Dockets Management System (FDMS) located at Regulations.gov. The system allows anyone to access FDA's administrative proceedings and rulemaking documents more readily, including *Federal Registers*, petitions, supporting documents and comments.

## Comment Period

Publication of a rule in the *Federal Register* officially opens the comment period. During this phase of the rulemaking process, agencies accept public comments via Regulations.gov. Some agencies also accept comments by mail, fax or email. The address for submitting comments always will be given in the notice. In a typical case, an agency will allow 60 days for public comment, although some comment periods have been as short as 10 days or as long as nine months. An agency may receive anywhere from no comments to thousands. Weekends and holidays are included in the comment period.

Some public comments contain one-sentence or one-paragraph comments, while others contain thousands of pages with detailed analysis and supporting documents submitted as attachments.

## Final Rule Stage

After the comment period closes, the agency reviews all comments received and conducts a comment analysis. It then decides whether to proceed with the rulemaking process or issue a new or modified proposal. In some cases, the proposal is withdrawn.

## Preparing a Final Rule

Any final rule must include a preamble and the rule text. The preamble includes a response to the significant, relevant issues raised in public comments and a statement providing the rule's basis and purpose. Typically, agencies respond to all public comments in the preamble of the final rule or a withdrawn proposal.

## Published Final Rule

The final rule is published in the *Federal Register* and made publicly available in print and online at www.federalregister. gov. No final rule becomes effective in less than 30 days from its publication in the *Federal Register*, unless it grants an exemption, relieves a restriction or shows "good cause," which includes such things as emergencies. A copy of any published final rule can be found on this site in the rulemaking docket, along with the relevant regulatory materials (e.g., supporting and related materials, public submissions).

## Guidance Documents

Draft guidance documents also appear in the *Federal Register* for comments. Guidance documents represent FDA's current thinking on a topic. They do not create or confer any rights for or on any person and do not bind FDA or the public. A company can use an alternative approach if the approach satisfies the requirements of the applicable statutes and regulations. If a company disagrees with the guidance document, it can use

the comment period to submit its objections to the proposal www.fda.gov/ RegulatoryInformation/Guidances/ default.htm.

## Regulatory Agenda

Twice a year, in the spring and fall, each agency publishes a regulatory agenda (also known as the unified agenda or semi-annual agenda). The regulatory agenda provides information about regulations each agency plans to issue or recently has completed. Individual entries contain a variety of information about each rule, including:

- brief description (abstract) of the rule
- timetable showing any past or projected actions in connection with developing the rule
- contact person for further information
- potential effects of the rule and related matters

To find the most recent version of the regulatory agenda, please see: www.reginfo. gov/public/do/eAgendaMain.

The regulatory agenda is important in allowing a company to plan for issues coming in the near future, their impact and documents it plans to comment during the year.

As part of FDA's Transparency Initiative and FDA Transparency Results Accountability Credibility Knowledge Sharing (TRACK), the agency also provides periodic updates on FDA's unified agenda rulemakings. On the Unified Agenda–TRACK Web page, FDA maintains an updated agenda of its unified agenda rulemakings www. fda.gov/RegulatoryInformation/ RulesRegulations/ UnifiedAgendaofRegulations/.

CHAPTER 18

# How to Comment

## What is commenting?

Commenting provides the opportunity to participate in the rulemaking process and shapes agency practice and policy that can affect the industry. These comments can influence the agency to modify its proposed rule or guidance document and are governed by the general administrative procedures under 21 CFR Part 10.

## Why does FDA ask for comments?

As a regulatory agency, FDA publishes rules that establish or modify the way it regulates foods, drugs, biologics, cosmetics, radiation-emitting electronic products and medical devices.

By law, anyone can participate in the rule-making process by commenting in writing on rules FDA proposes. FDA routinely allows time for public input and carefully considers these comments when it draws up a final rule. FDA gathers public comments mainly through two channels: proposed rules and petitions.

FDA files all comments in a public docket, and the information submitted also is available to anyone who requests it (while the document is still open and after the review period is closed it can

be viewed under the docket number on Regulations.gov or after it is archived it can be reviewed via the *Freedom of Information Act* [*FOIA*], so companies should be prudent in their comments since they are a matter of public record).

When FDA plans to issue a new or revised guidance or regulation, it places an announcement in the *Federal Register* on the day the public comment period begins.

- "Notice and comment" rulemaking is governed by legal standards of fairness and impartiality that are set out in the *Administrative Procedure Act* and apply to substantive rulemakings by federal agencies.
- In the notice and comment process, all parties stand on equal footing before the agency.
- The agency must consider all comments in its decision-making process and must respond to all comments when issuing its final rule.

## Where are items for commenting found?

Regulations, guidance documents, petitions, etc. that have been posted by the

**Figure 18-1. Commenting Flow Diagram**

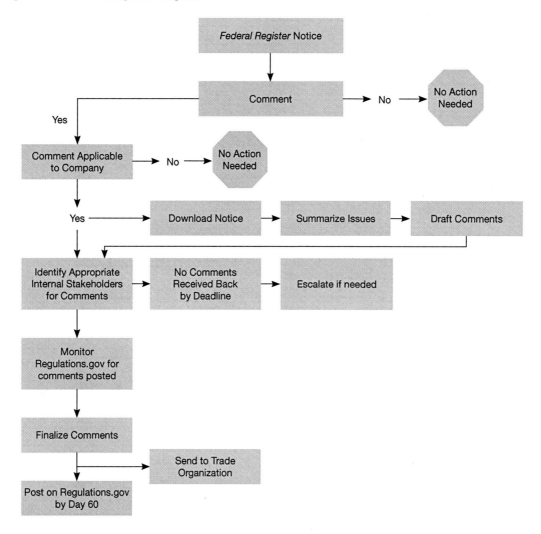

agency for comment can be found by reading the daily *Federal Register* or using any of the search functions on the Regulations. gov site (or by reviewing the dashboard feature on FDA's *Federal Register*, which summarizes all documents that are still open for comments: www.federalregister. gov/agencies/food-and-drug-administration ). Documents accepting comments are listed with the "comment" icon and the date the comments are due. Once a comment period closes, the comment icon is removed. The date may remain, depending on the agency's individual settings.

### Regulations.gov

Federal regulations have been available for public comment for many years, but people used to have to visit a government reading room to provide comments. Today, the public can share opinions from anywhere on Regulations.gov (www.regulations.gov/#!home).

Regulations.gov removed the logistical barriers that made it difficult for a citizen to participate in the complex regulatory process, revolutionizing the way the public can participate in and impact federal rules and regulations.

## Suggestions for Submitting Comments

There are four general areas in which companies may wish to comment concerning regulations:

1. The need for the rule—In the preamble of a proposed rule, the agency describes the need for the rule. If a company agrees or disagrees with the agency's explanation of the health, safety or fraud issue addressed by the rule, it can comment on that. The comment should be as factual and detailed as possible.

2. Other options—If the agency has proposed or discussed requirements, the company may be able to think of other things the agency could do that would solve the problem in a less costly way for it or industry. One option that has been suggested often is for the agency to give small firms more time to comply with a regulation, such as a change to the safety requirements or electronic publishing. Another option may be for the agency to identify a goal companies must meet, but to allow each firm to achieve the stated goal in its own way. A third option may be to request an exemption for certain types of businesses for which the requirements are not applicable. Because the quality and persuasiveness of the company's comment affects the agency's decision, including data, logical reasoning and other information to support the comment always helps.

3. Benefits of the rule—Due to an executive order, the agency is required to estimate the benefits of each proposed and final rule. This requirement might mean, for example, estimating how many lives would be saved or illnesses averted by causing an industry to change manufacturing practices. The company may want to explain (in detail if possible) whether it thinks a specific requirement would achieve the intended results. For example, it may want to provide detailed information documenting whether the industry has a particular problem. Furthermore, it may want to comment on the degree to which a proposed requirement is already common practice, and how much a federal rule would change practices in the industry. Finally, the company may want to comment on how a proposed regulation would benefit it through reduced costs or increased revenues.

4. Costs of the rule—In many cases, the regulatory options and costs of the rule will be the areas the company will know most about and may want to include in its submission. Under the executive order, the agency must consider the costs of the rule to the entire industry.

## Comment or Do not Complain About the Outcome

Why would a company comment? To be able to influence the outcome of a regulation or guidance document in a way that industry can implement in a practical way.

Public participation matters, too. Democratic, legal and management principles all underscore the importance of public comments and the significant difference they can make in regulatory policy. Public participation is an essential function of good governance. It enhances the quality of law and its realization through regulations (e.g., rules).

## When does a company comment?

A company comments when the guidance, regulation or legislation directly affects its industry or a particular segment of its industry.

The RI department should monitor the *Federal Register* on a daily basis, looking for opportunities to comment on legislation that affects the company if that is included in the department's goals or metrics. When a docket asks for comments, the RI professional should:

- assess the notice for applicability to the company's products and practices
- determine whether to comment via associations or organizations or individually
- identify internal stakeholders (if needed) to provide comments
- coordinate the internal commenting process and collate comments if more than one person is providing comments
- manage timelines for comment due dates and submit comments and supporting documents to Regulations.gov

Note, comments should be coordinated and submitted by one group. It is embarrassing and a matter of public record if two different subsidiaries of the same company submit opposing comments.

## Company Goals for Comments

The company goals and intended outcome for comments include stating the company's position using simple language, the rationale for its position, support for that rationale and alternative proposed text or position. All comments become public, so the company should be careful of its comments (be factual and unemotional).

## Planning for Commenting Throughout the Year

Twice a year, in the spring and fall, FDA publishes a regulatory agenda (also known as the unified agenda or semi-annual agenda). The regulatory agenda provides information about regulations the agency plans to issue.

FDA's agenda lists all the rulemaking proceedings that are planned, underway or recently completed. Individual entries contain a variety of information about each rule, including:

- brief description (abstract) of the rule
- timetable showing any past or projected actions in connection with developing the rule
- contact person for further information
- potential effects of the rule and related matters

To find the most recent version of the regulatory agenda, please see www.reginfo.gov/public/do/eAgendaMain

FDA's regulatory agenda is important in allowing companies to plan for issues coming in the near future and their impact, and documents on which it plans to comment on during the year so the RI professional can be proactive in planning, lining up experts and developing a position on the issue rather than being reactive when the rule/guidance document is issued in the *Federal Register*. This type of information is not available in all countries.

## Subject Matter Experts: Why They Are Needed and Where to Find Them

When commenting requires a particular expertise, the company needs to identify employees who are willing to help with comments so it can tap into their expertise. Sometimes this means creating an internal social network of experts (this is important in large companies) or understanding how each top-level employee can contribute (in a small company). To facilitate a quick turnaround of comments, it always helps to identify these individuals in advance.

## How to Help an Assigned Commenter Provide Comments in a Timely Manner

If an assigned commenter has not provided comments in a timely manner (by Day 45 or 50), the problem can be addressed in several ways. The company can advise the commenter that this is a priority and ask him or her to comment as quickly as possible. It also can identify an alternate expert to comment or draft a response and provide a copy for the commenter to review and edit since editing is always easier that initially drafting a response (if the company position is known).

## Comment Directly to FDA or Through a Trade Association

Depending on the regulation or guidance, commenting could be:

- directly, through FDA
- indirectly, through
  - o trade organizations
  - o scientific societies
  - o nonprofit organizations
  - o consultants
  - o law firms
  - o healthcare facilities

Commenting through a trade organization provides anonymity for the company, especially on a sensitive subject. This also means comments need to be collated and submitted to the trade organization much more quickly than if the company were submitting them individually, since the trade organization needs to collate the comments and submit them on time. A downside of submitting through a trade organization is that it will submit only comments that represent the industry majority or consensus position. While the company's comments will be anonymous, the trade association's submitted comments ultimately might not be the company's position.

Some companies, to ensure their comments are representative of their positions, submit through a trade organization and individually.

## Commenting Tips

FDA prefers (and in some cases mandates) comments be submitted online. Following are some other suggestions for ensuring comments have the greatest possible impact:

- Indicate clearly whether the company is for or against the proposed rule, or some part of it, and why. FDA regulatory decisions are based largely on law and science, and agency reviewers look for reasoning, logic and good science in comments it evaluates.
- Refer to the docket number listed in the *Federal Register* notice and specify page, section, and line the company is commenting on (it helps to develop and use a template for this).
- Include copies of articles or other references that support the company's comments.
- Submit only relevant material. If an article or reference is in a foreign language, it must be accompanied by an English translation verified to be accurate. Translations should be accompanied by a copy of the original publication.
- To protect privacy when submitting medical information, the company should delete names or other information that would identify patients.
- Spellcheck.
- Submit by the deadline; comments must be postmarked, electronically submitted or delivered in person by the last day of the comment period—the comment periods close at 11:59 PM ET on the date comments are due.

## Tracking

How is legislation that becomes proposed regulations, guidance documents, Citizen's Petitions (see Chapter 14) and agency meetings tracked so the company knows when to submit comments, implement a new requirement or attend a meeting? A daily subscription to the *Federal Register* and visiting the document management system on Regulations.gov will facilitate this.

The company can keep up-to-date on what other companies, groups or individuals are submitting comments on and their perspectives on the proposed rules by visiting that docket number on Regulations.gov.

Also, an internal spreadsheet or database by docket number (or topic) and due dates can be used to keep track of comments to be made (expected documents/legislation within the year), comments submitted and outcome of comments on final document issued.

### Format for Commenting

There is no special style for submitting a comment by mail or in person. If the comment is written legibly or typed on standard 8-1/2"x11" paper, FDA can process the comment more effectively. However, experience has found that the most efficient approach is to submit comments in a tabular format with FDA's proposed text and the company's response to the text next to it.

### Where to Send Comments

Details of where to send comments and background information can be found in the *Federal Register* notice.

### How long is the comment period?

Comment periods typically last 60 days. Some comment periods have been as short as 10 days or as long as nine months. Weekends and holidays are included in the comment period.

### When are comments really due?

The comment due date indicated on Regulations.gov is based on Eastern Time. For example, if the comment due date is listed as 05/05/2014, it is due by 11:59 PM ET that day.

## What happens when a comment is submitted?

When a comment is received, it is logged in, numbered and placed in a file for that docket. It then becomes a public record and is available for anyone to examine at Regulations.gov or in FDA Dockets Management's reading room (5630 Fishers Lane, Rm. 1061, Rockville, MD 20852).

## What happens after the comment period closes?

The agency reviews the comments. How quickly the review take place depends on agency priorities, resources, complexity of issues in the document, number of comments, issues raised by comments, etc.

Working groups review comments, and internal agency meetings are held to address specific issues raised by comments. Another draft of the document is prepared to reflect the response to the comments and includes all comments. A "final" draft document is circulated for clearance, similar to the process for the draft document, or a final document is issued and again published in the *Federal Register*.

## What are the possible results from consideration of comments?

- document is never finalized or is withdrawn
- document is modified
  - o changes with the final regulations can be seen because comments are addressed in preamble
  - o guidance silent as to comments, but changes can be seen
- new document is initiated
- comments noted, but no changes made

**References**
Linda Bowen, Slides for Regulatory Intelligence—Commenting, RI Course, Temple University, 2011

# CHAPTER 19

# Trade Associations

## What is a trade association?

While a professional association represents the people in a specific profession in an industry, a trade association represents the industry itself—specifically, the companies that comprise the industry, not the professionals who work for them. The trade association is formed to further the collective interests of the industry in negotiating with governments, academia, healthcare systems, advocacy groups or other organizations and is funded by the companies that operate in that professional field, typically through membership dues. It also is the trade association's responsibility to represent the industry to the public.

An industry trade association participates in public relations activities, such as advertising, education, political donations and lobbying (influencing public policy), but its main focus is collaboration between companies and government organizations. It also can issue guidelines and codes of ethics to which all members should adhere.

## How can RI interact with a trade association?

A trade association can assist RI professionals with their jobs in the following ways:

- legislation creation, tracking and influencing the outcome
- commenting (letting the company maintain anonymity) on policies, regulations and guidances
- representing the industry at public meetings and in the media

## Data a Trade Association Can Provide

Data a trade association can provide to an RI analyst include:
- publications on hot topic analysis or white papers
- topic-specific forums or blogs
- newsletters
- speeches
- fact sheets
- profiles and reports

## Trade Organizations of Note

While there is no specific regulatory or RI trade organization, there are a few representing the drug, device and biologics world including:
- Advanced Medical Technology Association (www.advamed.org)

- Biotechnology Industry Organization (BIO) (www.bio.org/)
- European Association for BioIndustries (EuropaBio) (www.europabio.org)
- European Federation of Pharmaceutical Industries and Associations (EFPIA) (www.efpia.org)
- European Medical Technology (www.eucomed.org/)
- Federation of Pharmaceutical Manufacturers' Associations of Japan (www.fpmaj.gr.jp/)
- International Federation of Pharmaceutical Manufacturers & Associations (www.ifpma.org)
- Pharmaceutical Research and Manufacturers of America (PhRMA) (www.phrma.org)

CHAPTER 20

# Professional Associations

## What is a professional association?

A professional association usually is a nonprofit organization seeking to further a particular profession and the interests of individuals engaged in that profession; it supports the people in that profession.

Many professional associations seek to develop and train their members, create educational programs; inform members of hot topics through blogs, journals, daily electronic newspapers or newsletters; offer ways to connect members; and certify that a member possesses and maintains qualifications in the subject area.

## How can RI interact with a professional association?

Typically, professional associations are not involved in shaping legislation or the regulatory environment, but instead, provide a platform for professionals to learn, network and exchange ideas and information.

## Data a Professional Association Can Provide

Through newsletters or publications, professional associations can provide actionable intelligence in terms of current legislation or hot topic information and analysis. They can provide blogs or forums in which to discuss the hot topic or ask questions to learn from the experience of other professionals who contribute to the site.

Educational programs that provide both networking and relevant information are another benefit, since an RI professional is only as good as his or her RI network.

## Regulatory Professional Associations—US

RAPS—Regulatory Affairs Professional Society (www.raps.org/)
DIA—Drug Information Association (www.diahome.org)
PDA—Parenteral Drug Association (www.pda.org)

### US Regional

RMRAS—Rocky Mountain Regulatory Affairs Society (http://rmras.org/)

North Carolina Regulatory Affairs Forum (www.ncraf.org/)
Orange County Regulatory Affairs Discussion Group (www.ocra-dg.org/index.php/en/)

## Regulatory Professional Associations—ex-US

TOPRA—The Organisation for Professionals in Regulatory Affairs (www.topra.org/)
BRAS—Belgian Regulatory Affairs Society (www.bras-org.be/index.htm)
DGRA—Deutsche Gesellschaft für Regulatory Affairs (www.dgra.de/english/index.php)
ARCS Australia Ltd. (www.arcs.com.au/About-Us.html)
CAPRA—Canadian Association of Professionals in Regulatory Affairs (www.capra.ca)

CHAPTER

## How to Set up an RI Department

### What is needed to conduct RI?

No matter the size of the company, an RI department can be organized, even on a shoestring. What is the bare minimum needed to set up an RI department?

- a willing person with good research skills and an understanding of the regulatory environment (with at least five years as a generalist)
- a computer with an Internet connection
- additional databases and subscriptions are nice features; however, these may be limited at smaller companies
- an RI toolbox (See Chapter 2 The Basic Regulatory Intelligence Toolbox)

### First Things First

However, if a more complex department is desired, factors that need to be taken into consideration include:

- Who will perform the function (will it be part time or full time)? It would be best to find a person with excellent research skills (this cannot be stressed enough).

- What are the RI professional's job description and overall responsibilities?
- What is the yearly budget?
  o What tools will be purchased for the function (databases, websites, consultants, etc.)?
  o To which journals should the company subscribe and where will they be kept?
- What will be monitored? (See Chapter 5 Monitoring and Surveillance)
- How will new information be evaluated against prior information?
- How will new information be integrated into current processes?
- How will new regulations, forms or guidance documents be distributed?
- What are the expected deliverables?
  - How will work be communicated to stakeholders?
  - How will work be stored and managed?
  - How will job function and output be measured (metrics)?

Small companies that have one person conducting RI part time, and large companies with dedicated departments of 3–15+ all have similarities and differences as illustrated below. And while all of the above need to be addressed to set up an RI department, how each company addresses these issues can vary widely based on experience, deliverables and budget. However, the RI process, no matter what the company size, is still the same.

## Small Company RI Structure

- RI professional needs to be more creative and flexible.
- RI professional depends more on colleagues (network) and consultants.
- RI professional needs to do more with less, due to limited resources and tools.
- RI is only part of the job function; therefore, there are more distractions while performing RI function.
- RI professional needs to know information quickly, as development programs are dynamic.
- RI is performed only when a question is asked or a topic needs to be researched (such as how to file a CTA in Canada, Australia and the EU).

### Small Company Advantages

- RI professional can move quickly and nimbly from topic to topic depending on day-to-day needs.
- RI professional needs to be more creative in developing both search strategies and final regulatory strategies, since smaller companies usually do not subscribe to items like Martindale: The Complete Drug Reference or the Physician's Desk Reference to complete a competitive label analysis (need to search FDA's site)—this also could be a challenge.

### Small Company Disadvantages

- fewer resources as medium and large companies
- may not have an electronic system to help archive or store information; usually a manual process
- due to time constraints, the RI professional cannot dig as deeply or research as extensively as he or she might prefer because day-to-day maintenance regulatory work also needs to be completed

## Large Company RI Structure (and Advantages)

- dedicated, experienced team to perform the wide range of RI functions
- work load divided by therapeutic area and/or region for each RI analyst
- multiple RI tools and databases used to efficiently perform, communicate and manage RI output
- knowledge management databases bought or created to manage the wide variety of regulatory information
- intranet or SharePoint portals for company wide information sharing
- well-honed processes, forms and maintenance procedures for RI activities
- RI performed on a daily basis, which therefore enables the company to catch issues that affect product development or approved products immediately and implement change
- for some projects, able to dig deep and provide in-depth RI coverage and analysis
- dedicated affiliates to help conduct surveillance and provide relevant information

## Small Company Resources

- utilize free resources (See Chapter 2 The Basic Regulatory Intelligence Toolbox)
- publications such as the *Pink Sheet*, *Gold Sheet*, etc., and others
- free email newsletters such as FDLI SmartBrief
- free email alerts such as FDA daily and weekly alerts, RSS feeds from health authorities
- *Federal Register*
- books
- courses
- RI databases
- consultants ,
- blogs
- websites such as RAinfo.com or Regulatorium.com
- journals such as *DIA Forum* and magazines such as *Regulatory Focus*
- regulations and directives posted on a health authority website
- guidance documents
- previous FDA reviews and available public assessment reports
- FOI requests
- Google Translate

## Large Company Tools

Includes all the tools used by small companies, plus:

- RI databases (with added features like cross-country tables, explanatory documents, Advisory Committee summaries, etc.)
- other databases such as PharmaPendium, CiteLine's Pharmaprojects Martindale, etc.
- NERAC (conducts focused citation searches)
- competitive business databases, market research reports and competitive intelligence databases

## How to Manage and Store Data and Data Requests

RI output must be managed, stored and shared. For small companies, an intranet site (such as SharePoint) is an effective way to manage and share data, including requests. Larger companies can employ an intranet site and databases (in-house, custom or off-the-shelf) and have more efficient systems for managing information requests, fulfilling requests, posting hot topics and distributing new regulations or guidance documents.

### Intranet/SharePoint Site

What typically is contained on an intranet or SharePoint site? To make it useful for users, the following content has proven, at a minimum, to be the most useful (a link on the home page to the site and then a separate page for each topic):

- "What's New" tab where you either post the most recent regulatory agency updates (by country) or include links to the past few published newsletters; also include a link to the newsletter main page with previous issues
- links to RI database and any other databases or RI tools available company wide
- "Hot Topics" section where links to recently published "Hot Topic" summaries are displayed
- research requests—including instructions for the request, the request form; also can include past, popular requests (Note: this typically is separate from the actual research questions database because unless it is a popular request it is necessary to ensure the information is current before someone accesses the request again as information might have changed in the interim)
- drug approval/summary basis of approval/public assessment report summaries—this is a summary of recently approved drugs and a database of previously summarized drugs by therapeutic area and class
- therapeutic area background— strategy, articles on the topic, competitive analysis, past

product review information, drug approval/summary basis of approval summaries (if not included elsewhere), presentations, etc.
- regulations by country (if maintained separately from the RI database or could be a link to the RI database home page that lists the countries)
- guidance documents, summaries and guidance interpretation library— a listing of guidance, by subject, by country with respective summaries and company interpretations/applications to current practices
- Advisory Committee pages— divided by therapeutic area, this page will include past Advisory Committee meetings (background documents, summaries and Advisory Committee meeting member profiles)
- trainings and presentations library (typically organized by subject and then by category within subject)
- reviewer and inspector profiles— listing by name of all reviewers and inspectors and links to their profiles
- commenting—this page can contain the items on which the company would like to comment (or is in process of preparing comments); a dashboard for legislation the company would like to affect (based on the regulatory agenda or other documents issued by health authorities to let companies know what will happen in the upcoming year); a list of those items on which a company has provided comments (and outcome if available); experts who can help with commenting and providing a company position for commenting; and an archive depository for all past comments submitted, by country

- FOI requests—the form to complete to request FOI documents, sometimes metrics on how many requests have been made, previous requests and its status (Sometimes this page also provides a link to an FOI/ Summary Basis of Approval/ Public Assessment report database where previously requests documents are stored and can be retrieved (or linked to an RI database that provides this feature)).
- enforcement/inspection databases— inspector profiles can be stored here as well as Warning Letters, inspection outcome reports and GXP trending information
- standards library (for medical device or combination device companies)
- articles—this can be a link to reference managing software or can provide articles the RI department consider to be of interest to the department, development team or company that do not fit under the scope of a therapeutic area or hot topic
- forms library—a central repository, by country and then topic, of the forms needed for submissions
- submission templates— a central repository, by country and then topic, of the templates needed for submissions
- links page—regulatory agency home pages and other pertinent global information
- "How to use this site"—instructions for what can be found on the site and why the user might need the information
- metrics information for RI department
- contact information for affiliate offices and RI personnel, with their respective responsibilities

## RI Department Budgeting

When considering setting up an RI department, a budget needs to be developed to include:

- basic costs
  - human resources
  - tools
  - infrastructure (computers, intranet, filing structure, databases, etc.)
  - cost sharing, if any, between departments
- annual vs. onetime costs for subscription fees and tools

## Expected Deliverables

To be able to budget for department setup costs, the roles and responsibilities need to be defined. A five-year plan can be created, outlining what tools will be purchased and what output will be expected for years 1, 2, 3, 4 and after full implementation in year 5, and how performance (justification for the budget) will be measured.

## Proposing an RI Department to Management

To recommend adding an RI function to company management, a proposal should be prepared that outlines the features of the RI department, its value and expected impact on the company, tools needed and budget. The key is to show the most value for the least amount of money.

## How to Demonstrate Value to Stakeholders

RI frequently is conducted within a company, and its value is recognized, but establishing a formal department can be challenging because it means a formal recognition of the work and a budget for tools. To help establish a department, the RI professional should outline the expected deliverables, hold informational meetings with internal stakeholders (departments) that would benefit from the data provided and get their perspective on the information needed. Showing them the benefits of an RI department should help gain their support. Once there is an understanding of what all the departments need from an RI department, the department can be proposed, with cost sharing on a trial and then long-term basis.

## Making the Case for Tools

Tools, especially ones critical to making the RI professional's life easier, can be expensive. It often is necessary to demonstrate the time saved by the use of the tools (vendors can provide this information), and time saving typically is significant (20–80+ hours saved). When the workload increases and the RI department is asked to do more work with the same number of people, tools are essential (the individual justification can vary but should be based on time and money saved). If a department is started with only the free tools, management should be made aware that productivity will be lower, as more manual work will be required.

# Index

## A

accelerated approval
    Fast Track designation, 26
    orphan designation, 26
    past precedents and, 42
    Priority Review, 26
    in regulatory strategy, 81, 83, 86
advanced notice of proposed rulemaking
  (ANPR), 108
advertising and RI, 4, 19, 117
Advisory Committee (AdCom)
    ADComm Bulletin, 18, 38
    expert advice, 59
    FDALive.com, 38
    IDRAC's ADComm Bulletin, 38
    information available before, 60–61
    information obtained from, 59–60
    meeting information, 61–62
    members of, 62, 63
    reviewer bibliography, 63
    RI output on, 5
    summaries of, 21, 62
    Tarius' SAC Tracker, 38
advocacy groups, 106
alert services
    Google Alerts, 37
    Google Translate, 37
    Mention, 37
    RSS feeds, 36
    TalkWalker Alerts, 37

approval packages
    European Public Assessment Report
      (EPAR), 11–12
    Summary Basis of Approval (SBA),
      11–12
approvals and past precedents review
    approved drug summary, 42, 44
    for-fee tools, 44
    free tools, 45–46
    information presented, 41–50
    PharmaPendium for, 45
    precedence summary, 46–48
    template for, 41, 42
approved drugs, ex-US, 41
Australian Public Assessment Report
  (AusPAR), 41

## C

chemistry, manufacturing and controls
  (CMC)
    data for drug summaries, 43–44
    regulatory strategy and, 79, 81, 83, 84
    in RI research, 24, 27
Citeline Pipeline, 44–45, 91
citizen's petition
    information necessary, 97–98
    processing of, 99
    reasons to file, 97
    submitting, 99
    supplementing or amending, 99

Citline. *See* Pharmaprojects; Trialtrove
clinical trial registries
    EudraCT, 10, 42
    IFPMA Clinical Trial Portal, 10
    JAPIC Clinical Trials Information, 10
    NIH Clinicaltrials.gov, 10
    WHO, 10
Clinivation Regulatory Intelligence
  Reports, 20
Code of Federal Regulations (CFR), 108
commenting, how to, 111–116
comments
    company comments, 113–114
    participation in FDA rule-making, 112
    processing of, 112
    submitting, 113
    through trade organizations, 115
Committee for Medicinal Products for
  Human Use (CHMP), 84
confidential information, IND and CTA,
  43
consultants for company type, 3
cooperative agreements, 73–75
Copernic Tracker, 37–38
Cortellis
    attributes of, 18
    drug summary, 44–45
    translations from, 74–75
Current Good Manufacturing Practice
  (CGMP), 71

## D

data processing, from surveillance, 39
Division of Freedom of Information
  (DFOI), 51
Dockets Management Office, 109
Drug Information Association (DIA)
    newsletter subscriptions, 36
    professional association meetings, 38,
     78
    regulatory intelligence defined, 1
    and small company resources, 123
    subscription database from, 12
    US professional association, 119
drug/device registration process, 5, 15, 19,
  83–84, 91–92
Drugs.com, 12

## E

*Electronic Freedom of Information Act
  Amendments*, 51
Emergo Resource Library, 20
Establishment Inspection Report (EIR)
    FOI requests for, 52
    for NDA review, 45
    PharmaPendium for, 45
EU RING (European Regulatory
  Intelligence Network Group), 2
European Public Assessment Report
  (EPAR), 41

## F

FDA
    Advisory Committees and, 21, 38, 59–62
    availability of reviews from, 49
    blogs of, 36
    citizen's petition and, 99–100
    citizen's petition to, 97–100
    comments to, 111–116
    developmental plans and, 31
    Dockets Management Office, 109
    electronic reading rooms and, 52
    FOI requests, 5, 51–54, 57
    hot topics from, 78
    information exemptions, 53
    informational websites, 11–12, 25, 45,
     48, 52, 91–92
    inspections, 71, 73–74
    interpretation of law by, 108
    law, 107
    marketing application reviews, 48, 88
    past precedents and, 41, 42
    Pediatric Study Plan, 95
    regulation by, 108–110
    regulatory information from, 15
    regulatory policy and, 104
    review teams of, 65–66
    strategy development and, 84, 87
    Transparency Initiative of, 110
    white papers from, 101–102
FDA Approval Packages, 41
FDA Voice (blog), 36

## H

health agency website precedence
  summary, 45–46, 49
health authority interaction, 104
Health Canada—Summary Basis of
  Decision (SBD), 41

## I

IDdb3. *See* Thomson Reuters Partnering
IDRAC ADComm Bulletin, 38
IDRAC® Cortellis. *See* Cortellis
information
  creation of actionable RI by, 2–3
  external to company, 4
  goals of analysis, 3
  internal, 4
  interpretation of, 10
  mining for RI, 4
  regulatory intelligence from, 1
  transformation to intelligence, 4–5
information sources
  commercially available databases, 9
  compared to "intelligence" sources,
    16–17
  differences for company type, 3
  networking, 10
  underutilized or undiscovered, 10
  websites, 9
inspection tracking and inspector profiles,
  71–75
inspections
  compiling data on, 75
  cooperative agreements, 73–75
  Current Good Manufacturing Practice
    (CGMP), 71, 71–72
  databases for, 72–75
  Good Clinical Practice (GCP), 71
  Good Laboratory Practice (GLP), 72
  outcomes of, 3
  WHO and, 74–75
inspector profiles
  information for, 75–76
  relevance to company and product, 75
Inteleos, 12
intelligence. *See* regulatory intelligence (RI)
International Clinical Trials Registry Portal
  Current Controlled Trials, 10
  WHO, 10
international non-proprietary name (INN),
  11, 26, 43

## L

labeling
  approvals and precedents and, 41, 50
  citizen's petition and, 97
  databases and, 19
  regulatory strategy and, 84, 86, 91
  RI research and, 3–4, 24
laws
  interpretation by FDA, 108
  origins of, 107–108
legislation
  as hot topics, 78
  influence on, 105, 113, 113–114
  pending or recently passed, 17
  professional associations and, 38, 119
  RI tracking, 3, 22, 115–116
  trade associations participation, 104,
    117, 119
  types of, 107–108
  white papers and, 101, 104
lobbying, 104–105

## M

MediRegs, 18
Memoranda of Understanding (MOU), 74
Mention, 37
monitoring and surveillance, 33–39
  *See also* surveillance

## N

National Archives and Records
  Administration, 108
NDA Pipeline information, 11–12, 12, 89
networking, 6

## O

operations responsibilities for RI, 77–78
orphan drugs, 42

# P

# Q

# R